ITALY AGAIN AN.

An Enthusiast's T:

BRIAN DARWENT

With illustrations by the author

ISBN 1.899310.28.2

British Library Cataloguing in Publication Data
A catalogue record for this book is available from The British Library

First published 1998 by
HORSESHOE PUBLICATIONS
Box 37, Kingsley, Warrington,
Cheshire WA6 8DR

Printed and bound in Great Britain by
Delmar Press Ltd
Nantwich, Cheshire

PREFACE

I have a friend, Florence V Dunstall of Shoreham, near Sevenoaks - known as Floss to her circle. Floss and I have never met and have only spoken twice on the telephone in the six or seven years of our friendship. We are postal friends, writers of private letters, a practice which must be close to dying out. I inherited Floss from Jack Trevor Story, although she may feel that *she* inherited *me*. We both at any rate used to exchange letters with Jack, himself a compulsive letter writer and surely the only professional author in literary history to have been willing to maintain a correspondence with just about anyone who would keep up their end. We only knew of one another's existence from fleeting references in his wild, stream-of-consciousness outpourings.

In 1990 I began to write a biography of Story. He was my primary source of material, and fully cooperative until laid low by a prolonged bout of depression. His letters dried up. Floss and I were possibly his only two correspondents who cared much: I had a biography to finish, she couldn't stand to lose such a unique penfriend. We both kept after him and eventually he came back on stream. There had been something of a change of personality, however. He began to give me a very hard time with the book, telling Floss meanwhile that he was only doing this to try to improve it. But whatever his reasoning, I was soon ready to abandon the project altogether. I had picked up her address and now wrote to her, telling of my frustrations and intention. She then wrote to Jack, hoping to improve relations between us but also describing me as a "misery guts". He in his mischievous way passed her letter straight on to me.

We have been in frequent correspondence ever since, strange to say. She bullied me into finishing the book, but I have remained a misery guts, at least in my attitude to my writing projects. Since Jack's death in 1991, she has found a whole new purpose in life: to keep me at it. She knows that despite a full-page review in the *Guardian* and wonderful endorsements by Stephen Fry, George Melly and others, my biography flopped, but she won't allow such negative thoughts to touch her. In fact she seems convinced that I am a better writer than Jack ever was, and wants the world to know this.

Floss is now well into her eighties, but she still swims every day and is as active as her arthritis will allow. She has two sons, one a successful businessman, the other a musician and arranger who does television work for popular shows. She has moved in interesting circles: her friends include both Roger Moore and his wife of long ago, Dorothy Squires. Her mind is as bright as ever. Whereas I, many years younger, am running out of reading stamina, she can never find enough good books to read. Her letters, though written on lined pages torn from a small pad, are a joy to read - gossipy and full of life and humour. They remind me of Nancy Banks-Smith's television column in the *Guardian*. She is the *real* writer, as Jack Trevor Story himself recognised long ago; but as I've indicated, she has the opposite idea.

I publish the odd thing now and again, usually in literary magazines; but most of my writing goes unread - except by Floss, who enthuses over everything. She won't let me *think* of giving it up as a bad job. I only have to mention a vague idea for some, to me, futile project and she is urging me to buckle down without delay. That's how this book came to be written.

My wife and I spend our holidays mostly in Italy, have done so for nearly twenty years. I have also been there on business. In need of something new to write to keep Floss off my back, I hinted some little while ago that I might try my hand at my Italian memoirs. She wouldn't let the idea drop. Soon I found myself unavoidably hard at work on the book, sending it to her chapter by chapter as it came off the word processor. She was in heaven again.

I kept protesting that I was really no expert on Italy and the Italians; that I hadn't much to say, and certainly nothing new, about its art and history, food and wine and all the other things on which a travel writer might be expected to have opinions. Only having really been there as a tourist, I couldn't manage much more than phrasebook Italian and had never managed a conversation of more than about three sentences with one of the natives. None of this made any difference to Floss. The brilliance of my writing would more than compensate for these minor drawbacks, she seemed to think.

I also checked the bookshops to see what was currently available in the way of modern travel books on Italy. To my surprise there was very little: only two volumes by Tim Parks on his experiences living amongst the people of a small village near Verona, so far as I could see. The hugely popular Bill Bryson had visited a few parts of Italy for his European tour book *Neither Here Nor There,* I also discovered. I thought his travel writing might be the right model: just try to be entertaining, don't bother with a lot of tedious research. I asked Floss what *she* thought.

"Forget Bryson!" she advised by return post. "Too smutty. And anyway, you're a better writer than he is."

Brian Darwent
Frodsham, Cheshire
October 1997

For my wife and daughters, with love.

BY THE SAME AUTHOR
ROMANTIC EGOTIST: An Unauthorised Biography of Jack Trevor Story
THE NEW SAROYAN READER (editor)
SAROYAN: MEMOIRS (editor)

CONTENTS

CHAPTER 1

CASTIGLIONCELLO - 1978

I first got to Italy on a "jolly", or semi-recreational business trip, back in the good old days of the late seventies. We were booked into the Mon Hotel in Castiglioncello, a more impressive establishment than it sounds and certainly better than I was then privately accustomed to. The trip would involve visits to a nearby (though thankfully not *too* nearby) chemical plant, but that seemed incidental. I remember well one moment on the afternoon of our arrival. We were leaning against the terrace rail, looking down at the sea and rocks below, when a senior chemist in our party who was on his third or fourth visit broke the stillness by asking rather puzzlingly what was missing. I had been thinking the scene, with a hazy sun hanging over a tranquil sea, lacked nothing. The only responses, after some head scratching, were of the usual male kind: booze, female company and such. (We were all men, which seemed less strange in 1978 than it would today.) Our colleague shook his head. He then drew our attention to how incredibly *quiet* it was, bearing in mind that this was after all a coastal spot. Still no one could guess what he was driving at. We listened to the silence in vain. One of us might have been tempted to give him a kick, but he at last relented.

"No birds," he said. "The feathered kind."

And it was true. Absolutely no bird life was to be seen or heard. Our chemist's theory was that the Italians had shot, snared, netted or otherwise caught and eaten their entire bird population! Whatever the truth of the matter, it was a chilling idea and an odd introduction to Italy, disturbing one's romantic feelings about the country. There was some scepticism, however; or anyhow a readiness to indulge in a little idle banter and speculation on such a pleasant afternoon. It wouldn't make much sense for hunters to *exterminate* their quarry, someone pointed out, because they had the next season to consider. There had to be a different explanation. Someone else noted that we would soon be into November, so the birds may only have flown south for the winter. A third idea was that the absence of bird life just here might be caused by pollution from the neighbouring chemical plant. There was no evidence for this - no dead birds floating in the water - but the suggestion did raise an ironic laugh. Not that we thought our Italian friends might be especially negligent: we simply knew something about such plants, wherever they might be located, and this was before environmental concerns had really caught on. "Aren't there supposed to be seagulls over Sorrento?" another voice enquired. And so it continued, as the sun began to redden and sink from view...

1978 does not seem so long ago, but it was also a much less fearful age. Business and politics were still dominated by the need to appease the trade unions, which had its agreeable side. Working for a big company, you felt extraordinarily safe and secure. The visit - financed jointly by the Italian company and our own, personal expenses included - was perceived by most of us almost as a holiday. It was my first foreign business trip, too, but I felt largely empty of gratitude. To spend a week in this rather splendid seafront hotel seemed no more than what the world owed me. And the freedom to comment on the scene in any way I chose was a basic right.

I doubt that many English people will have heard of the resort of Castiglioncello, delightful and memorable as the name is. (It remains my favourite Italian place name all these years later.) It is situated on a small promontory about twenty kilometres south of Livorno (where Shelley was drowned), on the coast of Tuscany. I have a tourist brochure, presented to me by someone on that first Italian trip. The Mon Hotel is easily visible in a number of (bird-free) photographs, standing imposingly above the rocks. I think we may have had the place to ourselves; leastways the tiled floors used to echo. I remember, too, first encountering *grissini* there (bread sticks for nibbling before a meal), an event that has lodged in my mind despite their insignificance as a food. Although the strip of sandy beach is rather limited, it is evident from the photographs that Castiglioncello attracts beach-loving visitors in the summer months. I have only been there off-season.

It was explained to me, I dimly remember, that the brochure was only a kind of mock-up. At any rate, though never used in any practical sense, it has quite literally fallen to pieces. There is only a single page of text, though in several languages. The English translation has some interesting turns of phrase. "The promontory," we are told, "reaches out into the sea with such impetus that it seems almost like an island. Castiglioncello's two worlds are accurately formed: the nether and the farther. This promontory juts out into the Tyrrhenian Sea, in the centre of Italy, and becomes a bathing and climatic resort. It is in the sea and yet covered with pine woods and hills." The resort, one gathers, does not seek to attract mass tourism. It is a place to visit for its peace and quiet, for the sun and for the sake of one's health. The available activities are of the more leisurely kind. For example: "One may fish, and leave one's boat in either of the two small harbours and divert the restlessness of traffic into a variant of State Highway No 1." No mention is made of gun sport.

But Castiglioncello is not a place to mock. My wife and I last visited the town in 1989 and found it as picturesque as ever, if excessively quiet, since we were off-season again. I understand that Italian film stars and other celebrities live or have villas in the area, though they are of course difficult for an English person to recognise unless very famous indeed. We certainly failed to spot any.

Nor should I mock some poor Italian's attempt at holiday-brochure English. We are after all the most backward people in Europe when it comes to foreign languages, and I am no exception. That first visit to Italy came unexpectedly, so that I had scarcely had time to glance at a phrase book. I did not so much as know how to say "Good morning" in Italian. The company had its headquarters in France or Belgium, and I had heard it was the policy that all employees should speak the French language. I took this too literally and went about saying "Bonjour" to the kind of people who in England might be less than fluent in their own tongue. Even my French was hardly up to schoolboy standard. I was thankful, however, that the meetings were conducted in a mixture of French and English; French for more general purposes and English when the discussions became technical. Our best French speaker, a senior research manager, was also a strongly-accented Scot. It was a relief not only to the Italians but to his English colleagues as well when he switched to the French language.

I got the impression that the Italian management style was a good deal more authoritarian than back home. There wasn't the same freedom for everyone present to contribute equally to the discussion; the more senior people obviously felt they were paid to do the thinking, while the job of the lower ranks was basically to listen and take orders, with only an occasional nervous attempt to make a point. Later, when more hands were needed quickly on the shop floor, it seemed possible almost to summon them out of the brickwork. No one actually whistled, but the effect was as if they had. I have since noticed the same kind of thing in restaurants and hotels. Outdated hierarchies are surprisingly able to coexist in Italian culture with strong individual flair and style. In the surrounding town much of the housing was still company owned, I gathered, and tenanted strictly according to position.

But the senior managers were generous people, both to their visitors and themselves. They were anxious, too, for the partnership to prosper. (Only a few years later, as a new and more competitive business culture began to take hold with the arrival of the Thatcher revolution, the friendly relations and happy exchange visits would come to an abrupt and sad end.) We were taken twice to a splendid fish restaurant in Livorno, where I had baby octopus (and I mean in the plural) for the first time; and also to Pisa. I had only seen the tower standing alone in photographs (which do not exaggerate the inclination), and was surprised to find it closely associated (as a bell tower) with the cathedral and baptistry. Back then you were permitted to climb the inside steps and emerge onto the narrow galleries at each level. There was no handrail or parapet, so that to stand between the columns and peer down was a giddying experience, especially on the side where you could see nothing below because of the tilt. We bought the best gifts we could find for our wives at the tacky souvenir stalls (there were lace items of reasonable quality), and dined at open-air tables in full view of the world's most arresting landmark.

The Italians seem to do pretty well for public holidays. At any rate, in the middle of our visit an unanticipated day off occurred (a saint's day, I think it was). So three of us decided to drive to Florence. We knew next to nothing about Italy, geographically or culturally, it must be emphasised. When we looked at the maps we had some difficulty locating Florence. We had some sense of its importance, so this was very puzzling; but we couldn't reveal our extreme ignorance to our hosts, who had casually suggested the trip. The largest city in the region was evidently known as *Firenze* in Italian. Could that be Florence? In some confusion, we set off to find out.

Italian drivers are said to be mad. That was not my general impression then, nor on later trips (Naples excluded). I would say they are simply very skilful, which in practice means you are less likely to have a collision. Our chief concern during the long drive remained whether or not we were heading for the right place. To return having made such a fundamental error would be unthinkable. We stuck to the major roads and doggedly followed the Firenze signs. The city had its share of suburbs, which we negotiated with some difficulty (a persistent sign saying "*senso unico*" gave us most trouble, I recall), never quite knowing if we were getting close to the centre. The big problem was that we simply had no mental picture of Florence and its principal landmarks. I knew it was a place of art treasures, because I could remember having seen on television the floods of the sixties and the desperate efforts to save them; but I had no idea where they were housed. Eventually we found ourselves on a narrow road by a river (which I discovered later was the Arno), where we managed to park our small Fiat in a tight space with one wheel on the kerb. We wondered if it would be there when we returned. Just in sight happened to be the famous Ponte Vecchio, which looked vaguely interesting.

It would be nice to report that upon struggling from the car and wandering into the *centro storico* of this renowned city we were instantly overwhelmed by the splendour of its architecture, public squares, statuary and monuments. Sadly, it wasn't much like that. The weather was dull, for one thing. And our first wish was to find somewhere to down a few beers. We were technical men after all, not art connoisseurs. But with our thirst temporarily satisfied, we set about trying to take the place in, which can be difficult when you don't know what you're looking for. We wanted of course to be impressed, but the usual descriptions you take home from a strange city - beautiful, fascinating, quaint, awe-inspiring - wouldn't serve. Florence wasn't any of those things on that day. It seemed faded and gloomy, damp and oppressive, with an excess of heavy masonry. Michelangelo's David (not the original) and the other triumphalist statues in the main Piazza della Signoria were stained with bird shit (for the Italians do allow pigeons to thrive). The Uffizi Gallery, where we gathered most of the paintings were displayed, was closed for the day. We liked the Ponte Vecchio best - towards dusk, with hippy-type musicians singing and playing guitars in gentle sixties' fashion among the jewellery traders. Thanks to our sponsors we were able to afford a good meal, after which we left Florence earlier than intended. Just outside the city we were surprised to run into thick fog.

As we flew out of Pisa's small and in those days rather primitive Galileo airport a few days later I felt delighted to have had this opportunity to see Italy at someone else's expense, but at the same time somehow less than thrilled with the place. It wasn't my intention to hurry back with my wife and family. Back home in Manchester the autumn weather just happened to be magnificent. Sitting in the back of our chauffeur-driven company car (how pampered we used to be!) as it sped through the Cheshire lanes I thought the English countryside, at that moment in full autumn colours, vastly more beautiful than the parched Italian landscape we had left. But I had had my first taste of the country, and Italy works its magic through the subconscious.

CHAPTER 2

CASTELLINA MARITTIMA - 1979

One man stayed on to look after the piece of experimental equipment we had installed through its anticipated early teething troubles. During this extra time he got better acquainted with one of the Italian chemists, who spoke remarkably good English. It turned out that the chemist had an English wife, from Worthing. Their names were Roberto and Brenda Menicagli. They had lived for many years in a company house in the town associated with the plant, but had just finished building a villa in a small unspoilt village up in the wooded hills, about fifteen kilometres inland. The villa had a self-contained flat, created with the idea of accommodating holiday guests. These it was hoped might be English, for Brenda had always missed English company. That was the basic advertising message brought back by the colleague who had stayed behind. In a moment of good sense, I saw that the chance of a family holiday in Tuscany with these English-speaking people, in a remarkably central location for the principal places of interest, was too good an opportunity to miss. The home weather had meanwhile turned nasty, and somewhat to my surprise I was already beginning to miss Italy.

My wife and I happened to be at the stage in married and parental life where for our next summer holiday we could think of going abroad. Our two daughters were well beyond prams and nappies, though the younger one, Suzanne, was in point of fact only four. But we didn't much fancy joining the package-tour throng to Majorca or the Costa-del-Sol, much as the girls might have preferred it. For us a holiday abroad should be the authentic thing, or forget it. This chance to see a bit of authentic Italy had therefore come at just the right moment. The charge for two weeks in the flat was ridiculously cheap, but we would have our flights to pay for and would certainly need a hire car. They were expensive in Italy, because of those supposedly reckless drivers. There were also worries about how the girls would cope with Italian food and such, for Italian restaurants were not then so common in England and they hadn't yet experienced it. But we were ready to put such considerations aside. In fact the decision to go was not, I regret to say, a democratic one taken by the whole family. We phoned the Menicaglis and booked a fortnight towards the end of the following May (before it got too hot) without really consulting the girls. Suzanne was obviously too young to comprehend, while Rebecca, then almost nine, would quite sensibly have voted for Blackpool, or its Spanish equivalent.

Italy! The idea of going there could grow on you when you had time to savour the prospect. My business visit had been too rushed, and of course time for real exploration had been very limited. Now we had four or five months to prepare. In the event this mostly took the form of dreaming, however, for we did little more than buy a phrasebook and a map by way of practical preparation. Rebecca, I imagine, must have suffered a little at school. She may even have kept our holiday destination a secret when others were talking about the delights of Benidorm or Tenerife. As for the prospect of Italian food, as typically stressed parents we did occasionally stoop to remarks like: "If you can't manage to eat sprouts, goodness knows what you're going to eat in Italy!"

Flights to Pisa from Manchester used to be difficult to arrange. In the spring of 1979 we had to travel down to Luton. My chief memory there is of observing Suzanne striding proudly out to our plane, swinging her small item of hand luggage. Whatever her thoughts on Italy, she had no fear of flying. Nor had Rebecca. The same could not quite be said of their parents.

By the time our evening flight touched down it was almost dark. We had a hire car already booked. Once in it, our sketchy directions were to ignore Pisa itself and instead follow signs for Rome. These would lead us easily to the S206, which we must then simply follow south. After about thirty kilometres we would see signs for Rosignano Marittimo, to the right. These would tell us it was time to turn left, to Castellina Marittima, which wasn't then signposted. Roberto would be waiting for us in the square in his car, ready to guide us up to the villa. Italy must already have begun to take possession of us, for we faced this last stage of the journey with surprising equanimity. And in fact the directions proved to be adequate; but what we hadn't allowed for was the possibility of encountering a major road incident on the way. Scarcely out of Pisa, we hit a solid jam. A vehicle had left the road (sometimes Italian drivers can be a little *too* skilful) and rolled down a steep embankment. Floodlights had been set up and rescuers were dealing with the injured. Police meanwhile were talking urgently to drivers at their windows, evidently suggesting they turn around and take another route, for some were attempting to do that. We decided to sit tight. This was a chance to use the most useful expression in the phrase book: "*Non capisco.*" ("I don't understand.") It served us well. While others were harangued, we were left alone, and then given priority when the traffic was at last able to move. (Having young children in the car I'm sure also helped.) But with the delay we got to Castellina very late. Roberto was much relieved to see us; as indeed were the villagers themselves, we were told later. Many were still outdoors, where the greater part of Italian life is happily lived. They were very pleased that "the English" had come to no harm.

Roberto Menicagli turned out to be that rare species, a red-haired Italian (due to a recessive gene which comes out occasionally in his family). He is in my experience a perfect gentleman, however, who is not in the least excitable, never mind bad-tempered. Brenda was a forceful personality with strong opinions; one of those Englishwomen abroad who have had to learn - and quickly - to speak and act assertively simply in order to survive. She still had a noticeable Southern English accent which, we noticed later when we heard her addressing locals or talking on the telephone, tended to carry over into her grammatically precise Italian speech.

We hardly knew where we were until next morning. They both worked down on the coast and had left by the time we were fully up and about. The villa turned out to be a kilometre or so outside the village, a gradual uphill climb. It stood in an elevated position, with marvellous sweeping views to the rear, almost to the sea. There was some land, including a small vineyard which sloped away steeply in the coastal direction. New visitors were presented with a carafe of the Menicagli's own brand of *Chianti*, which was perhaps a little on the rough side (we were no experts), though you very quickly developed a taste for it. The flat itself - at ground level, opening onto a rough patio area - could not be described as roomy, but as we anticipated doing little more than sleeping and cooking in it that wasn't a problem. Our waking time would be spent almost entirely in the open air.

After breakfast (we had brought a little food with us and the Menicaglis had provided bread) we set off down into Castellina on our first shopping expedition. It was already quite warm. There wasn't so very much to the place - a couple of streets, a square, a few shops, what we took to be a tiny town hall with a square little clock tower, a petrol station, bars and post office - and you could have said it was a bit shabby. But it was certainly authentic Italy. Most of the old men were already sitting outdoors, where they would seem to spend the entire day. We were viewed with a certain amount of interest - the girls especially, who were both fair-haired and fair-skinned - but nothing was said. No one, we realised, spoke a word of English. The odd thing was that we hardly appreciated how conspicuous we were. I had a phrase or two ready as we stepped nervously into the *alimentari* to buy groceries:

"*Buongiorno, signora. Sono inglese.*"

"*Buongiorno, signore. Sono italiana,*" the Italian lady replied, quick as a flash, smiling either in welcome or amusement, we couldn't tell. Our plan to persist with complex Italian failed us at that point. Shopping instead became chiefly a matter of pointing and using simple nouns - *patate... pomodori... pane... formaggio...* - which of course is all that is needed in order to acquire food in Italy and stay alive, provided you have the money to pay. This had to be taken from our palms, however, since the larger Italian numbers all sounded to us something like *cinquecentocinquecinquantacento.*

After a visit to the *fruttivendola*, and the awkward purchase of *francobolli per l'Inghilterra* from the post office, we were standing around taking a breather when we were approached by an aged Italian with iron-grey crew-cut hair and nutbrown sunken features, wearing a dusty dark-blue suit. He was strangely excited about something and began to jabber in Italian. We could only look at him in puzzlement, protesting with our favourite phrase that we couldn't understand him; but he seemed to have no idea that there were people in the world who did not speak his own tongue - either that or he believed that the language difference ought to be no obstacle if his message was sufficiently urgent. At length he indicated by gesture that he would like to buy Rebecca and Suzanne ice creams, and when we consented to this he calmed down a bit. In the end we simply had to walk away from him, with many repetitions of "*Grazie! Molte grazie!*" He looked worryingly forlorn as we gave him a final wave. Brenda and Roberto told us he was called Ivo. They thought him a character, but they didn't know anything about his background and couldn't imagine what he had been trying to tell us. The buying of ice creams became a little ritual each time we saw him in the village (sometimes we paid), which he appeared to enjoy. Ivo would still be around when we returned to Castellina the following year.

That first holiday in Tuscany was so successful and we managed to do so much that it is hard to know where to begin. In one single day, for example, we drove north through Pisa up to Viareggio and spent time on the beach (the sand was almost too hot to walk on), followed by rides in the park on the multi-seat bicycle contraptions; then visited the Torre del Lago Puccini, where the composer had lived and composed some of his best music; and finally, passing through Lucca, which had a real medieval feel to it, drove to Collodi, home of the Pinocchio industry. There was an entertaining theme park, which was as near as the girls were going to get to Blackpool.

Driving eastward on another day we headed for Volterra and San Gimignano. Small towns in Italy are often perched on hilltop sites. Volterra is a good example of this. And typically, as you approach you imagine there is going to be a bypass (just in case you should decide to give it a miss), but find that the road instead winds its way all the way up and through the middle, with a similar tortuous descent on the far side. Volterra is very dramatic indeed seen from certain angles. On the north side of the town there have been numerous landslides over the centuries on account of the unusual geological foundations. Whole chunks of the town have disappeared. At present an ancient church, part of which collapsed a hundred years ago, stands on the edge of precipitous cliffs. Volterra is a good place to buy alabaster ornaments and such. We came away with a squat but stylish bird of indeterminate species. The only real birds we were seeing on these inland excursions were pigeons still.

San Gimignano was less well-known in 1979, I fancy, than it is today. In Tuscany it has become *the* place to visit. It may even have motorway links by now. We reached it then via more of the twisting minor roads which you had to negotiate to get virtually anywhere in Italy. It stands on comparatively level ground but is easily seen from a distance on account of its unique skyscraper towers. I'm sure it has been described before as a miniature medieval Manhattan. Today only five major towers still stand, together with a number of lesser ones. Once there were more than seventy. The towers were built for military reasons, one gathers. Prestige must also have been a factor, I would imagine. Towers do not strike me as particularly safe places to retreat to during times of strife, and life inside them must have been horribly claustrophobic. We found the streets reasonably free of tourists (in marked contrast to a return visit ten years later). How much of these towns was truly authentic it was hard to know. The buildings around San Gimignano's main Piazza della Cisterna, for example, looked just a little too clean and undamaged to be entirely genuine. But if they were in part fake, then the fakers had done a wonderful job. In the *duomo* were the most horrific murals I have ever seen. Though painted way back in the Middle Ages, the colours seemed surprisingly fresh and vivid. Depicted were scenes from Hell, with gleeful devils performing the most ghastly acts of torture and mutilation upon their stoical victims. I couldn't wait to get out of the place. One had thought of San Gimignano as a haven of tranquillity.

Meanwhile word that we were in residence at the "Villa Menicagli" had reached certain people down at the plant. I had been only a junior member of the previous year's visiting party, but the desire on the part of the Italians to maintain good contacts was such that one of their people, of a similar status to myself, was instructed to pay us a friendly visit. I could recall that when he had been over in England he had given the impression, largely through mime, of being a compulsive womaniser; so I was surprised when he arrived at the villa on our first Sunday as a conspicuous family man. I don't mean that he simply brought his long-suffering wife along for a day out - several generations of his family came up with him for the afternoon, including a grandmother or two. They all sat or stood out in the hot sun. None of them knew any English at all - nor any French for that matter, which might have helped. Even the man himself was pretty much confined to Italian. But we had wine aplenty, thanks to the Menicaglis (who had gone off somewhere for the day), and enough simple food to go round. So what might have been a social nightmare turned into quite a convivial impromptu occasion, even if the conversation was limited to the comparative footballing prowess of Kevin Keegan and others.

We were also invited (by telephone) to visit a somewhat higher ranking manager for dinner. His English was fair and while his wife couldn't speak it she did speak French, which we could manage after a fashion. They had a dark and handsome little boy of precisely Suzanne's age. With her golden hair they made a striking little couple, though they weren't together long enough to develop any means of communicating.

We had dinner a couple of times with the Menicaglis themselves, too, of course. Roberto was something of a hunting man. On the wall of their living room was a mounted wild boar's head. English attitudes towards such trophies have since changed, but at the time I took it in my stride. Nor was anyone else affected by it. The girls have since become vegetarians and might react differently now. Wild boar were quite common in Italy still, we were told, though we didn't see any on our walks up in the near-impenetrable woods above the village. About the only wildlife in evidence were small lizards. They sunned themselves in the vineyard and were easy prey for the local cats.

During our second week we drove to Florence. Having been a little less than inspired by the city on my first visit, I wasn't so tremendously keen to return; but of course it could hardly be missed. Instead of using the major roads we took the route through Volterra and Poggibonsi, and approached the city from the south. The weather was very hot and sticky, but we were in happy mood even so.

As we planned to stay the night we had to find a hotel, preferably one with a car park, which wasn't going to be easy. But we found a quiet street away from the centre and left the car there while we strolled into the city and looked for somewhere suitable. Now Suzanne at that time had a particular terror of two things: crocodiles and Hoovers. We were in the wrong part of the world for the former, but the first hotel we entered had a big old-fashioned Italian industrial-sized vacuum cleaner parked near reception. We were in the midst of negotiating a room when she spied it and let out a shriek. This brought the discussion to an abrupt end. Our sudden problem was far beyond phrasebook Italian to explain; we could do no more than withdraw, leaving the lady at the desk very puzzled but thankfully not particularly angry. She knew we were English. A few doors on we entered the Hotel La Gioconda, on the Via Panzini. It had a small car park at the rear. Happily this time there were no vacuum cleaners on view, so we hastily reserved a room before a maid could appear flourishing one. I then hurried back for the car, which I was relieved to find undamaged. The hotel had had a brush with history, we learned later. Once the Mona Lisa had been stolen and had eventually turned up there (hence its name).

We had been warned about gangs of young thieves operating on scooters in Florence, lifting bags from the shoulders of languidly strolling tourists. But as with the supposedly crazy drivers, this proved to be a myth in our experience. In the bright spring sunshine the city looked altogether more appealing than it had on my earlier visit. Somehow the girls managed to endure both the heat and our boringly endless inspection of all the things visitors came to see. We tried to provide relief by allowing them to feed the pigeons in the Piazza della Signoria. Unfortunately they were in aggressive mood and Suzanne became very frightened. To escape the pigeons and the heat we went into an exhibition of Leonardo da Vinci's anatomical drawings in the Pallazo Vecchio. As a technical man (though only by profession, which should never be the whole of anyone) I had long sided with Leonardo over Michelangelo as supreme Renaissance Man; but I found them a little disappointing. Viewing famous works of art for real can be a thrilling experience - you are seeing with your own eyes something a great artist drew or painted hundreds of years ago - but for me they have often looked better in reproduction. I think that can be especially true of drawings. But then on this occasion I was carrying Suzanne, who was still crying, as I tried to squint at the sometimes faint and tiny exhibits through their thick protective glass.

After Leonardo, we retreated to our hotel to rest and get ready to go out for dinner. The girls were taking very easily to Italian food. They even developed a taste for veal, which neither can bear to think about as adults. The great pleasure of the Mediterranean countries is being able to stroll around in the evening in light summer clothes without any thought of the weather. Even with young children we stayed out quite late. The hotel room proved to be about the noisiest we have ever tried to sleep in. It was hot, too (no air-conditioning, of course); but we were glad to be there all the same. We hadn't yet developed the routine middle-aged critical attitude towards all hotels, British or foreign, which everyone seems eventually to adopt.

In fact we decided to stay for a second night, which meant we would have sufficient time as non-experts to explore the rest of the city. We hoped to see the original David in the Academy Gallery, but we found it closed. This meant we also missed several of Michelangelo's uncompleted works, which in photographs had struck me as more moving than the finished pieces. We did, however, see the *Pietà* in the cathedral, which I thought confirmed this opinion. Already beginning to wilt again in the heat, we descended into the remarkably cool marble Medici Chapels, which contain some of Michelangelo's more sexually ambiguous works.

But I make no pretence of being an informed guide. I have been to Florence twice more since 1979, but am noting here only the things that have stayed in my mind from that particular visit. In general I find Italian art uninspiring. Much of it is too religious and too medieval for my taste, the minds of the people in the paintings too remote and difficult to read. We walked dutifully around the Uffizi and admired the Botticellis, but what I chiefly remember is that the place was a mysterious hit with the girls. They ran up and down the long gallery, pointing excitedly. Only later did we realise that they had been counting the naughty bits on the statues. Elsewhere I certainly saw the painting of the execution of Savonarola. The practice was to hang and burn people simultaneously. I have no fascination with such images - quite the contrary - but they do stay in the mind. Similarly, I haven't forgotten the statue in the Pallazo Vecchio of Hercules killing Diomedes. Considering that the latter has taken a firm grip on the most vulnerable part of Hercules' anatomy just prior to being thrown, it would be interesting to know how the great hero himself emerged from the terrible struggle.

Next morning before leaving we drove up to the Piazzale Michelangelo, from which there is a splendid panoramic view of Florence. We were also able to have coffee as we gazed out over the rooftops. I do find the distant view of Italian towns and cities so very appealing. We then drove westward, following the Arno, to Empoli; and from there it was only a short drive north to the village which has been immortalised in a name: Leonardo da Vinci. The place seemed a bit of a disappointment, culturally speaking, though maybe we didn't look hard enough. (I understand it now has a superb museum, with models of Leonardo's experiments and futuristic contraptions.) But in a beautiful field of poppies there stood a modest little monument - recently erected, by the look of it - with a plaque proclaiming the spot as the great man's exact birthplace.

CHAPTER 3

CASTELLINA MARITTIMA - 1980

The following spring we imagined we could return to Tuscany and simply pick up from where we had left off. There were many places we still wanted to see within easy reach of Castellina: Siena in particular, and the island of Elba, where Napoleon had been exiled. A train trip down the coast to Rome could also be contemplated, now that we were seasoned Italian travellers. But most of all we simply wanted more of the easy-going sun-blessed Italian life.

It was a late decision, however, and that brought our first problem. The flat at Castellina was proving very popular, so that when we finally got around to phoning, Brenda and Roberto could not accommodate us at the villa for two full weeks. We would have to spend the latter part of the holiday at their townhouse down on the coast, which they hadn't yet managed to sell and still used a little. It was almost in an industrial area. The prospect was less than welcome; it put us in the wrong mood for Italy right at the start. But we refused to be deterred and went ahead with the booking. We had imagined the flat would be ours for the taking.

And when we arrived in Castellina something else was wrong. It was precisely the same time of year, but the lovely weather we had felt sure would be there to greet us was altogether absent. Instead it was cold and wet. We even had to light a fire in the flat with brushwood (which the Menicaglis had thankfully provided) to keep warm. Italy just wasn't supposed to be like that. Meals had to be eaten indoors. The village itself had the appearance of being deserted, the old men apparently confined to their homes. Without the sun it looked far less attractive. We saw old Ivo flitting about once or twice, but he seemed preoccupied so we rather avoided him. It was certainly not the weather for ice cream. But we had our hire car and didn't mope for long. On our first Sunday we drove to Cecina (pronounced "Shayshina" in Tuscany), a little way down the coast from Castiglioncello, then on down to Piombino, from where we hoped to be able to take a ferry across to Elba, if they ran on Sundays. Happily they did. We decided - sensibly, as we imagined - to leave the car behind and explore the island by bus. The weather was overcast but dry, and the crossing a little choppy but quite bearable. In no time the boat pulled in at Portoferraio, a picturesque port built around two harbours. For once we had prepared ourselves for the visit by buying a guidebook. In particular we very much fancied visiting Napoleon's Villa dei Mulini, and his country house at San Martino. The bus meanwhile would take us through beautifully mountainous countryside, with the villages as ever perched charmingly on the hilltops. Alas, it was not to be. No public transport was available, it seemed. And we were told at the *ufficio informazione* that in any case Napoleon's houses were closed on Sundays, along with just about everything else of interest on the island. We had come on the wrong day, and out of season, too. *"Elba è chiusa?"* I offered, summing up for the lady. She nodded that that was the case. We didn't bother to try to get to the bottom of why the office itself had bothered to open its doors. There wasn't even anywhere we could see for coffee, so we simply remained stranded on the quayside until the ferry returned. So much for Elba!

The day wasn't altogether wasted, though; the abortive trip had only taken a couple of hours. With the weather showing slight signs of improvement, we drove further south to Grosseto, then north again on twisting minor roads through the hilly Colline Metalliferre region. The Italian landscape can be surprisingly green in spring and there is always an interesting village to stop and explore, with an adequate *trattoria* hidden away.

We spent the next few days in the Castellina area, travelling no further than the immediate coastal towns. The weather remained uncertain, but it was getting to be quite warm. One afternoon we were on our way back to the village when we passed a stout white-haired old man struggling to push his car. We drove on a little way, but then conscience compelled us to turn around and offer him a helping hand. Had we known that the heavy task we faced would be of the linguistic rather than the physical kind we might not have bothered.

When we got back to him we were surprised to see that he had abandoned the struggle. Even odder, though, was the fact that he was in no distress. He had the front door open and was sitting quite contentedly with his feet out on the road. He wasn't even mopping his brow. In this posture he would not have aroused our concern, but of course we knew he was an old man with problems.

He looked up as we climbed out of our car. I raised a hand in greeting and we asked as best we could if he needed help. It soon became clear either that he couldn't understand a word of what we were saying (not that there were many) or was deaf, probably both. This forced us to shout in our embarrassingly limited Italian, at the same time demonstrating our meaning by pretending to push our own car.

"Ah," he said, the fog apparently clearing. But he hadn't got the hang of it at all for he stood up and came across to help *us*.

"No. Questa macchina ha una problema, n'est-ce pas?" I shouted with great emphasis, pointing at and then patting his car. He remained concerned about ours, however, and was all for lifting the bonnet. He tugged at it but I refused to operate the release catch, whereupon he scratched his head and shrugged his shoulders. He was about to return to his seat when a basic question occurred to him - one that we understood. Where were we driving to?

"Castellina Marittima."

"Castellina!" He looked suddenly very pleased. With a couple of exaggerated gestures he indicated in triumph the direction of the village, then the way our car was pointing. But frustratingly for him we still weren't satisfied. Instead we stubbornly tried to drag the conversation back to the original topic - his car and our belief that it had broken down. Did he need any help - *assistenza*?

"Assistenza? Si!" He placed a fatherly hand on my shoulder and pointed up the road to a distant small garage. *"Assistenza!"* he repeated. *"Buono!"*

We could do no more. He resumed his seat and watched us drive on a little way then turn our car around. As we waved him farewell he was smiling broadly and giving us the thumbs-up sign. The episode would have remained a mystery had it not been for the fact that the Menicaglis by chance knew the old man. It turned out that his son owned the garage he had pointed out to us and he was simply waiting for him to come along. He was very embarrassed when the reason for our spirited attempt at intervention was explained to him. One mystery remained: how had he got the message through to his son? We never found out.

Once more the weather deteriorated. We were growing anxious about our planned visit to Siena, which would be easier to reach from Castellina than from down on the coast, where we would shortly have to move to make way for the Menicagli's next guests. We also wanted to go by train to Rome for a couple of days from the townhouse, and there wouldn't be time enough left for both trips.

With our last day at Castellina almost upon us, we decided there was nothing for it but to set off for Siena in the rain.

We were by this time no longer the happy English family that a little decent Italian weather would have made possible. I had had too much of the Menicagli's *Chianti* and was inclined to take the hairpin bends in more aggressive style than usual, my wife had a bad headache, and Suzanne was prone to travel sickness - which could also be traumatic for Rebecca if we weren't able to stop the car in time. Siena seemed an awfully long way, too, all the twisting and turning probably doubling the actual distance.

And throughout the journey the rain simply refused to let up. We parked the car near a church somewhere on the outskirts of the medieval part of the city, donned our cagoules and splashed our way in what seemed the sensible direction. All we really knew about Siena was that there was a colourful and exciting horse race called the Palio held later in the summer in the main square. We didn't have a street plan, but we thought this square, the Campo, should be easy to find. Before we reached it, however, we spotted a likely eating place for lunch and decided to spend an hour over a meal, in the hope that the rain would clear at last.

But if anything it seemed to come on heavier as we lingered over the food. At last there was nothing for it but to plunge back into the streets. We quickly located the Campo, which you could hardly miss since it was dominated by the Tower of Mangia, easily the tallest structure in Siena. For a small charge you could climb it. That seemed a good idea, chiefly because it would provide relief again from the weather. We were becoming seriously wet. The steps seemed endless, but the view from the top was quite magnificent, even on such a dismal day. We looked down at the vast semicircular Campo and tried to imagine the Palio in full swing - the dazzling costumes and banners, the deafening roar of the crowd, the snorting and thundering of the horses - but it wasn't easy. There was hardly anyone about. In the end, as with mountains, there was nothing for it but to make our descent. But just before we did Rebecca pointed out our little red hire car some distance away. It happened to be visible over the rooftops, by some accident of building alignment. I pretended to be interested, as parents do, but of course thought it of no consequence.

There was much more to see in Siena. Back at street level, we paddled on. The city used to have many towers, like San Gimignano, but with the exception of the impressive one we had just climbed they have disappeared. There has been little modern destruction, however, of the kind that has disfigured so many of our own urban landscapes. You find these old Italian cities miraculously all of a piece. The explanation may be that the nation hasn't been able to *afford* the wrecking costs. But a more likely reason is greater civic pride. Italy has more world-renowned cities than any other nation. They are more important in themselves. Even in heavy rain you could marvel at how miraculously well-preserved Siena was... Then Suzanne began to cry. It was all really too much - time to abort the visit. We would have to come some other time to have a closer look.

"Let's get back to the car!" my wife said.

I let her take the lead while I carried Suzanne behind. I am no good at retracing my steps anyway, and tend to rely on my wife. We walked on for some distance without speaking. I could tell she was angry, but apart from the general distress I didn't know why. Finally she stopped.

"Where is it?"

"What - the car? *I'm* just following *you*."

"As always."

"I haven't a *clue* where it is. I know we parked it near a church, but Siena must have a *thousand* churches."

"Well, you'd better find the right one - and quick! Look at the state of Suzanne! She'll catch *pneumonia* at this rate!"

"Maybe we should buy a map." I didn't wait but dashed into a handy touristy shop and bought one.

"*That's* a waste of money!"

"Hang on! Let me open it out!"

But my wife refused to look at it. And in truth all it did was confirm that Siena did indeed have a lot of churches.

"We'll have to take them one by one," I said with a shrug.

I set off in pursuit of this plan, with my bedraggled family following at a disbelieving distance. At the third or fourth, with the car not yet in sight, it was time for fresh thinking.

"Maybe it's been stolen," Rebecca said, trying to be helpful.

"No, it's the wrong church again, I'm sure."

"Then why have you brought us here?" my wife demanded. And even more unreasonably she cried: "I want to go home *now!* And I mean to *England!*"

"Don't be *hysterical!*" I shouted. "We've got to work through this problem patiently and rationally."

"You do that if you want, but take me *home first!*"
Then Rebecca said something, in a timid voice.
"What?"
"The tower."
"The tower? What *about* the bloody tower?"
"We could see the car from up there."
There was a moment's stunned silence. She had probably saved our lives.

I glanced at my watch - nearly five o'clock. "I bet it closes at five." We could see the tower easily in the distance. "Follow me down and wait outside!"

I splashed through the streets and managed to enter the building in the nick of time. "*Torre!*" I bellowed, slapping down a handful of coins. The man probably took me for a suicide, but thankfully he did nothing to restrain me. I leapt up the stone steps and at last reached the viewing balcony. And miraculously there still was our little car, over by a big church in the middle distance. I took a bearing, then having a breather looked down for the last time at the Campo below. I tried again to visualise the Palio, but my imagination was by now inoperative.

My family was waiting outside when I reappeared. "I'll be back with the car in two minutes," I said, racing past them. "Don't move!"

But when I reached it there was a new problem - of all people a traffic warden! He began to gabble.

"Shut up!" I bawled, forcing coins into his hand. He accepted them readily enough but wouldn't subside. I brought out notes and counted them into his open palm until silence was at last achieved; then I climbed into the car and screamed off in the direction of the tower.

But now I had forgotten that cars weren't allowed in the narrow streets around the Campo. I had to select a new parking spot and note its position again in relation to the tower. I also marked it on the street plan, and would have daubed arrows on the wet stones if I'd had a tin of paint.

Five minutes later I was carrying Suzanne safely back to the spot, with the others close behind. Munching chocolate that my wife had managed to buy, we left Siena without a backward glance. One day (it hasn't yet happened) we intend returning; but next time it will be to see the real Siena, in the blazing heat of a summer's day, with the Palio going strong.

Of course I needn't mention that as we drove back to Castellina the weather at last began to improve. For the rest of the holiday it was much like the previous year. On our last day there we ambled around the village, bought a little food and a few stamps, and had a pizza. There was a bar which doubled up as a small café where they did the most delicious pizzas we have ever tasted, straight from a wood-fired oven. (The first time we ever went in there of an evening with Roberto, the men had been so boisterous that we believed a serious row was going on which would at any moment turn into a fight; but it was evidently just ordinary Italian conversation.) Outdoors again we bumped into Ivo and were as polite as we could be while wishing to avoid deep conversation. But we did explain (or tried to) that we would be leaving next day - *domani*. He seemed very disappointed, which was simultaneously sad and puzzling.

In the late afternoon, after a brief *siesta* at the villa, I decided to drive down to the village again to buy petrol. I was surprised as I drove through the gates to find Ivo just passing by, and walking in my direction. We hadn't seen him up that way before. It would be polite, I thought, to offer him a lift. I opened the passenger door.

"Castellina?" I enquired.

He pointed ahead.

To avoid further misunderstandings, I got out and guided him towards the passenger seat. He seemed oddly reluctant to accept the lift and gabbled a little, but with gentle persuasion I got him safely into the car and closed the door. I couldn't understand why he looked so mournful about it. The journey - a stiff uphill walk of a kilometre or so in the other direction - took about three minutes. During the short drive Ivo several times referred to Rebecca and Suzanne. I explained that they were back in the villa.

"*Si, si,*" he said, nodding.

We reached the square and I deposited him at his favourite corner, giving him a final little wave. I had filled the car with petrol and was half way back, still feeling pleased with myself, when I realised what I had done. Though he had been understandably shy about it, poor old Ivo had walked up from the village in the hope of seeing *us* for the last time.

We moved next morning down to the townhouse, which turned out to be pretty basic, with a big stone sink in the kitchen, and curiously gloomy in spite of the sunshine; but comfortable enough. One thing that has really stayed in my mind is that hung around the outside walls were little wooden cages containing small birds. At first they struck us as rather charming, but then we realised the birds were probably for eating, once fattened. We never did get around to confirming with Brenda and Roberto that this was actually the case.

We had a day in Castiglioncello, where I hoped we might have lunch at the Mon Hotel, but it hadn't yet opened for the summer. Instead we spent time on the beach, which in late May was quiet. As a general holiday rule we like to avoid both the height of the tourist season and the hottest weather when we can, though it can sometimes seem like a mistake. We didn't fancy swimming, with the chemical plant only a few kilometres south, around the headland; but I do remember that on that day Rebecca at last achieved a full handspring. She had been practising all week, though with all the rain we had had, not exactly out of a sense of joy.

Next day we caught the train to Rome, a journey of more than two hundred kilometres. Italian trains can be unluxurious, though they have the advantage of being cheap. They also in my experience run on time, notwithstanding the permanently chaotic state of Italian governance since the days of Mussolini. (Usually, anyway.)

The Menicaglis and the tourist literature had said we should be especially wary of rogues of all kinds in Rome. This advice was strongly in our minds as we stood in obvious bewilderment in the middle of Termini station's vast concourse, wondering how to proceed. We might have tried to book a hotel in advance, but that would have been against the spirit of these Italian excursions.

Next thing we were approached by a very correct-looking little man in a dark uniform and peaked cap.

"You want hotel? Yes - no?"

"Yes," we confessed, though going on quickly to explain that we intended to find one ourselves. He didn't wait for this, however, but sprinted to a telephone. We saw him speaking rapidly into the receiver, haggling by the look of it. Then he dodged back through the crowd.

"I fix. Follow me!" he commanded. And with that he grasped our suitcases and marched straight out of the station at a pace our younger daughter couldn't hope to match. No police being around, there was nothing for it but to give chase. My wife and Rebecca dashed ahead, while I picked up Suzanne and struggled along behind.

Without flinching, the man crossed a wide and busy road and, eyes straight ahead, marched tirelessly onward into the unknown depths of Rome. The two in front managed to scramble across the road also, then Rebecca was forced to hang back, trying to wait for Suzanne and me without losing contact with her mother, a big responsibility for a nine-year-old. I managed to get Suzanne to the other side, then, strung out almost to breaking point, we rounded several corners and crossed a minor road or two, until at last the man set down our suitcases outside a nondescript hotel on the corner of a large square. Not once had he looked back. I saw everyone go inside, and by the time I reached the reception desk, with Suzanne in my arms still, a deal had been struck which I was in no condition to question. The little man raised his cap, gratefully accepted our small tip, then shot out into the square to return at a brisk trot to his hunting ground.

When we had recovered we found the hotel to be actually very pleasant, with a cool little courtyard, and remarkably inexpensive. Various tours we might take were mentioned, but when we indicated that we would prefer to explore the city on our own they made no fuss. As a bonus, from our window we had a view of the church of Santa Maria Maggiore, featured some years earlier in Kenneth Clark's *Civilisation* television series.

We were in Rome for two nights - one full day in the middle - which we have found is about right for seeing a city if you simply want a general impression without getting into too much close inspection. We were in certain respects limited, of course: night life wasn't high on our agenda with young children; dinner in a restaurant had to be the evening's entertainment. Nor were we in Rome for the shopping, or for religious reasons. We simply wanted to see what we could by day at a civilised pace and without benefit of a guide. Rome is the only major city we have visited where we have made good use of the buses. This was partly because we got into the habit of not paying. Not that we couldn't afford it; we simply never got properly to grips with how it was done, and in the meantime were certainly never challenged. For all practical purposes the buses were free. They took us everywhere, and at a reasonable speed.

The Colosseum was one of the first things we looked at - so huge that you didn't need an Italian phrase to ask where it was. A certain amount of reconstruction work was apparent, but the place was remarkably intact for a structure so ancient. You could wander along the alleyways through which the wild animals had passed below ground before emerging into the arena. My wife and I were both upset by it all, though for slightly different reasons. She felt it was a burial ground, and that to stroll around gawping was a sacrilege. I was more affected by the thought of the scarcely imaginable horrors that had been perpetrated there for public entertainment. One gathers that the animals, however hungry, were often as frightened as their victims, and sometimes had to be coaxed into action by having their living meals wafted temptingly under their noses.

The centrepiece of our middle day was St Peter's, which was an extraordinary experience even for an agnostic like myself. What struck me most was the astonishing *quality* of everything; there was nothing your eyes could rest on that did not look infinitely beyond price. Michelangelo's sculptures in Florence had left me surprisingly unmoved, but his *Pietà* in St Peter's (in its own chapel), a fully-finished piece, seemed to me just about the most exquisitely crafted object in the entire universe. The Sistine Chapel, by contrast - not at that time cleaned - was less awe-inspiring than I expected. Most casual visitors seem to marvel chiefly at the physical task involved in painting such a huge ceiling. I couldn't relate to it - all that concentration of bodies and religious significance. I remember better a carved lion somewhere in St Peter's that scared the wits out of Suzanne. I recall, too, sitting on a cool terrace under trees drinking coffee, with a clear view of the dome of St Peter's. And later I sat on the steps in the sun with a reverse view of the square and Bernini's colonnade and wrote a self-addressed postcard from Vatican City.

Elsewhere in Rome we sat on the Spanish Steps while Rebecca, already showing musical talent, coaxed a tune from a simple little wind instrument she had bought, and a man made brooches of the girls' names from twisted gold wire. We also threw coins in the surprisingly compact Trevi Fountain, as would be expected. The remains of ancient Rome in the Forum were somewhat meagre, requiring a great effort of imagination to bring to life, though the guidebooks had helpful artists' drawings of how it had all once been. We got more entertainment, though, from observing the numerous lizards. But there was no disappointment in our visit to Rome. We walked and gazed and stopped to eat and drink and rode the buses, and had a great time. There was a little further trouble waiting for us at the station, however.

We got to Termini in good time for our early evening train. It soon emerged, though, that we could have stayed in town and enjoyed a leisurely dinner. No train appeared. Slowly we gathered from the lack of activity, and from the comments of fellow travellers, that some sort of wildcat strike had blown up. No information, written or spoken, was provided. We were furious, but to our surprise the continentals accepted the situation with a shrug of the shoulders. At last a station official appeared. He took up a position close to us, but we waited in vain for a word of explanation from him. He simply stood motionless and silent, staring down the track to where the rails disappeared in the gathering dusk. No one questioned him. I made a few loud and sarcastic comments, and when these failed to provoke a response decided to confront the man.

"*A che ora il treno?*" I asked succinctly.

No answer.

I tried for greater eloquence: "*Il treno non partenza - perchè?*"

Still no response; not even a movement of the eyes.

Infuriated, I searched my mind for cutting phrases, but could only achieve spluttering movements of the lips. I was considering physical expression when a bystander spoke to me in French. Slowly the explanation penetrated. The man wasn't *permitted* to communicate with the public; it was part of the strike. I sat down with my family again, feeling wiser, though no less impatient. But then after a few more minutes the rail system sprang suddenly back into life, with everyone scurrying about and talking loudly as if nothing had happened.

CHAPTER 4

VENICE - 1984

We decided to leave Italy alone for awhile in the recession of the early eighties. My company went through a downsizing exercise which at the time seemed cruel but was mild compared with the later experience. I survived by simply ignoring appeals for voluntary heads. Meanwhile we economised with holidays in England. But Tuscany we felt we had covered pretty thoroughly as casual tourists, and we weren't sure where else in Italy we wanted to go. The Menicagli's flat was getting to be too cramped for us as well, now that the girls were growing. We were beginning to need a little more comfort. And there were other European countries to consider for holidays. Italy certainly exerted a pull, but we hadn't yet reached the stage of needing our annual fix. Our next visit wasn't planned. In 1984 we booked a package tour (finally weakening and accepting the convenience) to Rovinj, on the Istrian peninsula in Yugoslavia, and discovered we could have a day in Venice at modest cost.

But Rovinj itself was almost Italy. Istria had been under Italian rule until the end of the war and Rovinj was reckoned to be the most Italian, in both culture and appearance, of its coastal towns. In fact I found it every bit as visually appealing as most of the Italian places I had so far seen. That was becoming my own first holiday priority. The hotels were set in pine woods through which you walked to reach the shoreline, passing old ladies in black displaying their lace produce. From that approach the town, with its twin harbours full of small craft of all kinds, and the backdrop of the old town clustered around the hill topped by St Euphemia's church, looked to be just about perfect. In fact I was so affected by it one morning that I took Suzanne (then aged nine) aside and tried to persuade her to appreciate the beauty of the scene. I know I used the word glorious more than once, because the girls still sometimes have a giggle over the incident.

In some other respects Rovinj in those days might have been considered boring. The few shops were pretty uninspiring. They mostly sold filigree jewellery and were uniform and controlled. Only the ice-cream vendors acted as if they cared about pleasing their customers. They were in fact developing the selling of ice-cream into a stage act and were fun to watch, though you didn't always feel entertained when they deliberately smeared your hand with it as you bought one. There were plenty of restaurants, and we like to eat out quite a bit even when staying half-board; but the menus and prices were all the same, so that it didn't much matter which you chose. They also provided a little unexpected entertainment, in connection with a certain bean-like green vegetable which I can't identify but which we quickly christened "the green thing". You only ever got one, but it was never missing from the plate, no matter which of the standard dishes you ordered. The green thing had the most revolting taste imaginable - like *poison* - but the odd thing was that few people seemed to recognise and avoid it, even locals. We loved to watch the dishes arrive at the nearby tables and the diners begin to tuck in, happy and relaxed - until the moment when the green thing was at last picked up on the fork and placed in the mouth. Chewing would proceed as normal for a few moments; then it was time to watch the diner's face. It used to remind me of a Ken Dodd TV sketch years ago featuring a supposedly traditional Lancashire game in which the contestants had to bite deeply into a peeled lemon, marks then being awarded for face control and endurance, timed by stopwatch.

We had to be at the landing stage very early for the Venice trip. You then got St Euphemia's church in silhouetted side view, with the sun behind, and saw that it was much too big for the hill from that angle. You could also reflect on its bell tower, said to be modelled on the Campanile in Venice itself, though this was going to be difficult to verify because we had heard that the original Venice tower had fallen down about seventy years before.

The crossing was at high speed, but it would take about two and a half hours. Having succumbed to the package tour, we found we were now going to have to put up with a guide. I can't quite see why this seemed so intolerable at the time. We would after all only be in Venice for a matter of hours, so it was as well to know something in advance. And in the event we soon felt a little better disposed towards the man; either that or we were growing lazy. He spoke in at least four languages, very fluently and seemingly off the cuff, though it must all of course have been well-rehearsed. While still affecting disdain, I was secretly much impressed. I had seen the Canalettos, and so had some idea of what to look for through the slight mist; but the direction of our approach meant that no familiar view presented itself, though we were in sight of land - odd bits, anyway - long before tying up and disembarking. Then our guide clapped his hands, raised his blue umbrella, and marched us firmly in the direction of the Doge's Palace, the Bridge of Sighs and St Mark's Square - the very places everyone was most familiar with and so most wanted to see. But we went along with it.

The month was August, so Venice was hot and crowded; yet there was no stink, as we had feared. The canal waters are a kind of smelly-looking blue-green in colour, but they were odour-free. I had to rely on my wife's nose for that. Mine is quite useless as an organ of sense, but hers is the keenest I have ever encountered, and Venice passed the test - much to my surprise and relief, I may say. We followed our man along the waterfront, crossing a number of bridges and passing souvenir stalls, until he stopped in front of the first important building.

No one would remember for very long much of his brief history of the palace, however eloquent and informative; but few of us would forget his breezy commentary on the Bridge of Sighs - which had no romantic associations, as we may have imagined, but simply joined the palace to the adjacent old prison and had had to be crossed by the prisoners on their way to a melancholy fate, their sighs reaching passers-by below. Next we stood in a huddle between the twin pillars on the waterfront (stolen from Egypt, we gathered) while he explained amongst other things that this was the precise spot where the state's higher-ranking enemies were put to death. We groaned a little ourselves. He knew his stuff, but St Mark's Square, just around the corner, was going to require a much longer lecture. We were being guided, meanwhile, to a designated restaurant for lunch at a pre-arranged time. It was time to rebel, which fortunately was quite within the terms of the excursion. My wife and I might have hung around for longer, but the girls had certainly had their fill. They were so far less than thrilled with Venice.

And I must say I can't understand why everyone congregates in St Mark's Square, anyway. Not that I know it at all well, but I have certainly seen it pretty often on TV travel programmes and in photographs. Whatever its historical associations, its appearance is of a vast military parade ground. You almost expect to see a parade of rockets and tanks passing through, as in Red Square of old. And when the expensive bars and restaurants put out their tables and chairs to tempt the tourists who have little else to do but feed the pigeons, they even arrange *those* in military formation. The buildings aren't particularly attractive, either. St Mark's Basilica itself reminds you of the Brighton Pavilion and is quite out of harmony with the rest of the architecture; the new Campanile looks as if it was built only yesterday and is equally discordant; and the rest of the surrounding buildings present for the most part unrelieved, unvarying facades, which are hardly beautiful. Yet everyone gazes in stupefied wonder. But it is possible to feel grateful for St Mark's Square. It strikes me as having a similar function to Windermere and Bowness in the English Lake District: that is to soak up the surplus tourists, thereby freeing the rest of the place for the enjoyment of more energetic, adventurous and genuinely appreciative visitors.

For having left the square, I quickly found Venice to be easily the most beautiful and fascinating city I have ever visited. (We made a return visit - again from Rovinj - in 1990, which confirmed this.) You simply have to get away from the crowds and wander in the quieter places - the backwaters, if you like - which even in August were available in abundance. There cannot be a more marvellous city for walking in. The total absence of road traffic is extraordinarily liberating for the pedestrian. In most cities, to put it simply, you daren't step back spontaneously to enjoy the view for fear of being run over. Enchanting vistas were suddenly revealed at every turn. Venice is a city to look at with the free eyes of an artist, in my humble judgment, rather than those of a scholar: facts and history are a distraction when every scene your eyes light upon is a living painting. And we didn't in truth have time for much else. We simply walked and looked, probably for at least a couple of hours. Then we noticed that the girls were not only bored, but hot and hungry, too.

We had little idea of where we were, though it hardly mattered. We found a small pavement restaurant for lunch. Once that had been a little adventure, but the girls were no longer so easily entertained. Rebecca was now fourteen and beginning to assert herself strongly as a teenager. To wander aimlessly in the heat, in a place devoid of pop music, where every single thing was old and boring, wasn't her idea of paradise. After the meal, having endured the usual parental lectures about what it had cost to bring her to Venice and how she ought to show more appreciation, she decided to go AWOL. It was reminiscent of her behaviour as a very young toddler, when she had liked to wander off, with no fear of getting lost, and would have walked on and on alone, into the sunset, if she hadn't been watched and followed. We used to experiment in the hope that she would get frightened. It hadn't of course been funny at the time, and nor was this now. But at least she had the sense to keep us in sight, even if we occasionally lost sight of her. Eventually we found ourselves close to the Rialto Bridge. My wife was growing especially furious, as Rebecca of course realised. She decided to cross the bridge to escape, and then thought better of it and waited defiantly at the crest for the inevitable severe ticking off - which at least happened in a memorable spot, as I hope she remembered to tell her friends when she got home. To calm things down we spent time in the shops on and near the Rialto and allowed the girls to choose souvenirs whilst we bought a small painting. Soon family harmony was more or less restored.

We had a final trip down the Grand Canal to look forward to, but hoped also to have a ride in a gondola. And unexpectedly we found this was possible at only modest expense - the only kind we could hope to afford. Just down from the Rialto, on one of the broader stretches, a sort of ferryman-gondolier was offering the experience of a ride on the Grand Canal *crossways*. Even more surprisingly, we didn't have to queue. And included was a generous pause in the middle for photographs.

But now we suddenly realised we were running late. Those who had left the guided tour had been sternly ordered to be back at the two columns by five or risk being stranded in Venice. Suzanne no longer needed carrying, as in past crises. We ran through a maze of narrow streets with only the sun for navigation, and we kept losing that. Venice is not a city to get lost in when you have a deadline to meet. In the end we were saved by little yellow signs guiding us somewhat haphazardly in the direction of *San Marco*. But on reflection it couldn't really have been so very difficult, for the square has another function: it's the only place in Venice that you cannot fail ultimately to find. Late in the day you only really need to follow the crowd. The more intrepid visitors all drain back to St Mark's Square towards evening.

We were not the only party visiting Venice that day, so the trip by launch along the Grand Canal was conducted at a stately pace as part of a long but quite colourful convoy. You got a different view again of the city, with all the palaces and expensive hotels and other grand buildings lining its banks. We did the full circuit, around by the docks, then cruised back along the broad Canale della Giudecca, passing close to the church of Santa Maria della Salute, which stands at the entrance to the Grand Canal. Although attracting fewer visitors than St Mark's, on account of its relative inaccessibility, it has probably been more painted and photographed. As we emerged from its shade there came into view at last the familiar Venice waterfront and skyline made famous by Canaletto.

CHAPTER 5

SORRENTO - 1986

For those more in love with the distant, scenic aspects of Italian towns and cities than their street life, Sorrento is the place to visit. Laid out in the sun on its extraordinary cliff-top plateau, beside a blue sea and with a shimmering backdrop of blue mountains, it looks magnificent. Arriving from Naples airport, this panorama is your first view as you climb out of Vico Equense and round the long bend to begin the slow descent into the town. It is also your last on the day of departure, and the probable reason - along with the prompting of the famous song - why so many visitors, straining for a final glimpse through the coach window, make a private vow to return one day to Sorrento.

The better known view is from the western end, however. The road, leading eventually to the Amalfi Drive after crossing the peninsula, climbs high above the Marina Grande (which back in the eighties was actually smaller than the Marina Piccola, but has since been developed), and provides the viewpoint for the picture you see most often in the guide books and holiday brochures. A promised land indeed!

This vision of an earthly paradise is not altogether fulfilled at street level, sad to say. But then how could it be?

Our holiday in Sorrento in the summer of 1986 was with friends. The girls came along, too, as did our friends' somewhat younger sons. We stayed at the Mediterraneo, in the suburb of St Agnello; which meant a hot, dusty and rather dangerous walk of a kilometre or more along the Corso Italia to reach the town itself. But the Mediterraneo was excellent - rather old-fashioned and situated well away from the busy main road, which is not true of many hotels in Sorrento. From the dining-room terrace, and from the bedroom balconies, too, if you leaned over a bit, we had a spectacular view across the Bay of Naples to Vesuvius. That seemed a great privilege, though of course there are few points on the bay from which the volcano cannot easily be seen. Visitors with a fear of volcanoes - hardly irrational - might find it difficult to relax.

One disappointment about Sorrento, at least as far as we were concerned, was that you quickly realised it attracted many English visitors. Strong links were evidently established during the war, following the landings at nearby Salerno. In some ways it's nice when foreigners genuinely try to make us feel welcome, and it can be equally satisfying to see ordinary English people - who a generation or two earlier could not have imagined ever reaching such a place - contented in a foreign setting. But the unavoidable fact is that you don't have to be very sophisticated to be put off by boards outside little cafés advertising egg and chips, full English breakfasts and the like. There were too many of these places in the vicinity of our hotel, one even offering "chip butties".

At first we thought we had stumbled into an English enclave; but then we had our first hazardous walk into town and were truly aghast to see a prominent yellow sign in the main Piazza Tasso, directing visitors to the "Rovers Return Inn". (When my wife and I returned in 1994 this at least had happily disappeared.)

The predominance of English visitors was also frustrating for fledgling students of Italian. Even the barest knowledge of the language just wasn't needed. Efforts in that direction could in fact cause irritation. You might launch bravely into a prepared sentence in a restaurant or shop, only to notice from a raising of the eyes to heaven and a sagging of the jaw that you were pushing the poor man or woman beyond endurance.

Apart from all this, we found Sorrento to be not an especially captivating place. The streets of the older part of town are for the most part on one level and laid out in a rather boring square grid, inherited from Roman times. True, there are any number of excellent restaurants, some with a terrace view of the bay and Vesuvius, and lots of good shops on the Corso Italia for those who travel to exotic places primarily for the shopping; but there is still something lacking. You can visit the museum, walk in the small park, spend time in the Foreigners' Club, or descend to the Marinas - the road down to the Marina Piccola, in the shadow of the precipitously situated Excelsior Vittoria hotel, is steep and spectacular. But sooner or later you realise this is not exactly an earthly paradise. Maybe too much of the place is too modern, for the average Italian shopping or housing development of the postwar decades is sadly no more alluring than its British counterpart. Whatever the deficiency, Sorrento is not a town that can keep you fascinated for very long. We had been told by our rep on the coach as we passed through it that Castellammare, just along the coast, might well be a hotbed of Mafia activity; and in the small coffee bars in Sorrento you did sometimes notice a lone customer who was inclined to whisper and was apt to be served without needing to pay. But that was a side of Italian life more or less invisible to casual visitors, offering little exercise for the imagination. In fact there could be no real contact with the local people, in spite of their excellent knowledge of English. You would have had to spend months there to gain much insight into what was really going on, and we had only two weeks. Pretty soon it was time for excursions to some neighbouring places of interest.

This idea wasn't popular with all members of our party, however. Our daughters had reached the stage of preferring to stay around the hotel when on holiday. They could now be safely left behind, and had more than had their fill of Italian sightseeing. The hotel had a good swimming pool and an outdoor pizza place where they could also buy ice creams and cold drinks, and so offered all they really wanted from holiday life - except perhaps for a little shopping - given that Sorrento had very little in the way of a beach. But we did manage to persuade them to come with the rest of us to Pompeii.

As elsewhere in Italy, you could get around easily enough by public transport and so hardly needed to sign up for any organised excursions. The railway station in Sorrento is a terminus - end of the line running around the bay from Naples. There is a convenient stop for Pompeii (Pompei Scavi). At the ticket office you could try if you felt like it saying, "*Vorrei otto biglietti per Pompeii, andata e ritorno, quattro adulti e quattro bambini, secondo classe, per favore,*" but the man might be unable to stifle a yawn while you were still in mid-sentence.

As for Pompeii itself, the chief thing I remember from that visit is the heat. We chose what may have been the hottest of a fortnight of very hot days, and the site offers little in the way of shade. If any roofs survived the day when tons of burning ash simultaneously buried and preserved the Roman settlement and its people, they were now missing. The sun was pitiless.

We had some prudish concerns, with children in the party, about the kind of images that might be on open display, given the hedonistic life the Romans were evidently leading at the time of the eruption and their reputation for illustrating their wicked doings in paint and stone. The general absence of this sort of thing as we staggered among the ruins was an unspoken puzzle, if also a relief. In the event we saw only one mural that would make you blush, and that mercifully somewhat hidden. Only late in the day, when it was almost time to leave, did a fellow day tripper whisper that all the choicest material was modestly hidden away in a building called the Villa of Mysteries, set apart from the rest of the site, and possibly only available for viewing by arrangement. In the circumstances, and given the fearful heat, we felt unable to follow up his lead.

Exploring the site was made much harder by the appallingly bad road surfaces. It seemed unlikely that they could have been reduced to this state by the feet of modern tourists; you could only think that it had been the same for the Romans themselves. Sprained or broken ankles must have been commonplace. In fact you wondered why they had bothered with all their arduous road building. In such a dry country ordinary dirt roads would have been almost as durable, much easier to create and maintain, and a good deal kinder underfoot. And if walking was difficult, a ride in an unsprung wheeled conveyance of those times must have been absolute hell. Better to be the slave or donkey doing the pulling, you would think, than the poor Roman dignitary having the life rattled and shaken out of him! You could actually see the deep ruts worn in the hard uneven stones and wonder at the years of jangled agony they represented.

The most recent eruption of Vesuvius was in 1944. This would have been around the time when World War II was passing through the area. The event must have been a strange accompaniment to the gunfire and other sounds of man-made death; enough to cause a religious conversion or two, you might guess. 1944 was within my own lifetime, so I found reassurances that the volcano was nowadays inactive not altogether convincing. In the Antiquarium at Pompeii you could see casts of people and animals caught in the moment when the deadly ash rained down. Even more chilling was the realisation that what had survived was not the bodies themselves but the spaces they had once occupied. And Vesuvius itself still loomed over the site, its huge jagged crater a constant reminder of its enormous destructive power. Yet there are modern settlements much closer to the volcano than Pompeii, which indeed looks to be at a safe enough distance!

Pompeii is really too big and too awkward underfoot to enjoy on a hot day. It is all rather uniform, too, in the sense that most parts of the site are preserved to roughly the same extent. My wife and I visited the less famous Roman town of Herculaneum by train on another day and found it to be on a more human scale (if I can put it that way). Herculaneum is closer to Vesuvius than Pompeii, and also closer to the sea, which was an escape route for some. It was buried by lava rather than volcanic ash and remained for many centuries undiscovered. Only in the present century has the town been significantly excavated, and parts are still buried beneath adjoining modern settlements. Because of the nature of its burial, Herculaneum is rather better preserved and more complete than Pompeii. The solidified lava not only prevented removal of material from the site by earlier generations of vandals, but also helped support the structures over many centuries, with the result that even some two-storey buildings have survived. One or two shops are extraordinarily well-preserved; much like they must have been two thousand years ago, though with not much in the way of goods for sale. All told the site seems to have more colour and warmth than Pompeii, and the roads are certainly in a far better state of repair. The only negative point I can recall is that the local neighbourhood is rather rundown and even menacing. Not that we came to any harm, but you are only just outside Naples, and the site attracts only a fraction of Pompeii's visitors. Waiting on the near-deserted station platform to return to Sorrento, with seedy apartment buildings uncomfortably close, we felt distinctly unsafe for the first time in our Italian travels.

No one was especially keen to make the full ascent of Vesuvius and peer directly into its gaping, sulphurous crater. But we didn't want to miss another much-advertised coach excursion - along the famously scenic Amalfi Drive, on the southern side of the Sorrentine Peninsula. Coastlines with rugged cliffs, deep ravines, a twisting road with precipitous drops at every turn, and villages clinging perilously to the hillside and tumbling down to small harbours and beaches certainly ought to be a delight to the eye. The problem can be getting the best angle. This one would not look at its most picturesque from a boat at sea, which must be the cherished viewpoint of the rich and famous residents of Positano and the other coastal settlements. It would all look rather flat, with the more dramatic features largely invisible. Nor would the scene from a plane or helicopter be an improvement, since hilly or mountainous landscapes tend to look more impressive from a lower level, which emphasises the skyline. Rugged coastlines are best viewed edge on, from a position on the coast itself. Happily this is the predominant view from the coach as you drive to Amalfi, at least if you are well-favoured in your seat position. So the casual tourist can have an actual advantage, if the beauty of the landscape is what's important. The experience would be even better from the front seat of a car, though maybe not for the driver, who would be much tempted - and exceedingly foolish - to allow his eyes to stray from the road ahead. The tranquil azure sea below is probably full of wrecks.

Our coach tour extended only as far as Amalfi, once a seaport of some distinction but now a beautiful if rather cramped tourist resort. This congestion is partly explained by the fact that the ancient waterfront has over the centuries disappeared beneath the waves. We took a local bus trip - a truly tortuous climb - up to Ravello. The town has a commanding position but was otherwise a trifle drab, as I remember it. I was partly intrigued because I had heard the writer Gore Vidal had a house or villa there, though in the unlikely event of meeting him I would have had to confess that I hadn't read his books, much as I admired the stand he had taken on various political issues.

The reverse drive from Amalfi, probably just as scenic, was inevitably less thrilling. And with less to hold your visual attention it seemed more uncomfortable, and more than a little scary (particularly after we heard a rumour that news had been suppressed of a coach recently going off the road and plunging down the cliffs). I have to say, too, that much as I enjoyed the excursion, nothing I saw compared with that intoxicating view again of Sorrento as we turned the corner to pass high above the Marina Grande.

Particularly visible from St Agnello, and even the Mediterraneo's dining room, are a number of hills topped by crosses. One of the more distant ones in particular looked to be an especially challenging climb. One hot afternoon while everyone else was enjoying a *siesta*, my friend Tony and I felt suddenly inspired to scale this arresting peak. We thought there was no need to consult a map - the hill was as visible as Mount Everest from base camp. We simply took a road in roughly the right direction, then changed to a path when a suitable one presented itself, and so wandered onward and upward, all the while deep in conversation about matters totally unrelated to what we were doing. The heat and the exertion probably made us a little mentally disorientated, too. After about an hour all we knew was that we were well up in the hills. Nowhere below looked recognisable; nor could we any longer see the distinctively-shaped hill we were supposed to be climbing. But we paid little attention to these things because our conversation had reached too interesting a point. I can't of course remember what we were actually talking about, but I do know that our never-ending debates and discourses are apt to proceed much as this walk was proceeding. We lose sight of the argument, approach things from a different angle, but none of it matters. We simply enjoy the verbal journey. Even so, we were sufficiently conscious of our surroundings to begin to have a very slight concern about the total disappearance of our objective. Then looking up we suddenly saw a cross, only a hundred feet or so above. Something extraordinary had happened, we believed. The reason we hadn't been able to see the hill was that we were already scaling it. And now the summit was within very easy reach. We didn't exactly shout for joy as we scrambled up the last bit; but we felt a mature satisfaction in our achievement, even if the view was less than anticipated. This wasn't something we could ponder for long, however; it was getting late. To return to St Agnello we had only to be able basically to distinguish north from south, and with continuous sunshine and knowing the time of day, even we could manage that. We made the descent in more thoughtful mood, however. Something seemed wrong. Later at dinner, looking at the hill from afar, we were puzzled still as to why we hadn't had better views from the summit. Afterwards we reluctantly looked at the map. It turned out that we had set out to climb Monte Vico Alvano, which is more than six-hundred metres high and is close to the southern coast of the peninsula, overlooking the Amalfi Drive - at least four kilometres from our hotel, even as the crow flies (if there were any crows in Italy). The map also showed us just how many more hilltop crosses there were in the region. We never did work out which one we had actually reached.

We saw no bird life up in the hills. As for seagulls, they were sometimes to be seen around the ferries, but appeared disinclined to venture inland. They were probably thankful for the protection of the Sorrento cliffs.

CHAPTER 6

PERUGIA - 1989

Some years had passed since we had been to Tuscany. By the late eighties it was becoming a very fashionable place to visit, and even to live for those who could afford it - an Italian Provence or Dordogne. I'm not sure when the word "Chiantishire" was coined, but it summed up what was evidently happening. Even for people like ourselves, well removed from the smart set, it could be a bit off-putting. We wanted to see Tuscany again, but then to explore less familiar regions. *Umbria* (further east) sounded right - a rich, sun-roasted kind of word, more flavoursome than Tuscany, or even the Italian *Toscana*. As far as we knew the partying crowd (not that we would be seeing much of them) hadn't really discovered it yet, at least not in any numbers. We would be able to visit our old friends the Menicaglis in Castellina Marittima again, and then drive on into unknown but highly inviting territory. Which is precisely what we set out to do at last in the late summer of 1989, leaving the girls at home (Rebecca was shortly to begin her second year at university).

One worry was the driving itself. My wife had lately become a very nervous passenger - largely attributable, we discovered after some years, to caffeine. She was seriously frightened of making the trip and no other country in the world but Italy would have induced her to do it at that time. I explained as reassuringly as I could that we were entirely familiar with the roads around Pisa airport - it was simply a matter of following the signs for Rome rather than Florence; then we would be safely on the S206 and driving down to Castellina in no time. I knew it would also be Saturday lunchtime, but I couldn't think that would make much difference. Maybe the roads would even be quieter.

The fact that Galileo airport had been considerably upgraded since our last visit ought to have been a clue. Doing my best to make the whole thing seem routine, I drove our hire car confidently out into surprisingly heavy traffic - and immediately saw to my dismay that the road system was now quite unrecognisable. Wearing a forced grin, I tried to concentrate on the imperative of following *Roma* and not *Firenze* when the choice presented itself, while at the same time wrestling with the difficulty of having to accustom myself instantaneously to driving on the right, something I hadn't done in nearly a decade (and the last time had actually been in New York). Then came the sign - and of course I had a directional blackout and off we sped towards Florence, trapped in a stream of cars from which there could surely be no escape.

I had never seen traffic like it in Italy. God knows what was causing it. And as we headed north into the city it became even denser, so that you thought gridlock must soon occur. That had only ever happened once in my experience - in Paris back in the late sixties during a rail and Metro strike. Many of the drivers had stood with their doors open, one foot inside, honking continuously. (We were fortunately only pedestrians.) In Pisa that day I almost saw it again; but the Italian drivers by contrast nonchalantly turned on a little extra skill and so kept things moving. There was virtually no honking, and certainly no danger to life; though my wife was not altogether receptive to that message. I've no idea how we extracted ourselves. Maybe I saw an opportunity to perform a desperate U-turn (which my fellow drivers would have taken in their stride); or perhaps we managed to reverse our direction by a more conventional series of right turns - my memory is a blank. But I do know that before long we had left the nightmare behind and were sailing in highly nostalgic mood down the Via Aurelia, as the S206 is more romantically known.

We were to stay the night at the Menicagli's villa. They took us out that evening to a favourite restaurant, which we imagined would be close by. In fact the drive must have been thirty kilometres - with the usual hair-raising hairpin bends, each one tighter than the last - through black country (for the days had already begun to shorten). I was fearful that my wife would have a complete nervous collapse, but to my astonishment she chatted merrily away to Brenda in the back seat while Roberto spun the wheel with one hand as the bends loomed up out of the night and casually asked me about business developments back home.

Next morning we had breakfast on their balcony, with that marvellous view over the small vineyard down towards the distant coast. Afterwards maps were spread out and a route planned which would take us eventually into deepest Umbria.

We set off first down the well-remembered road through Riparbella - a village that saw few tourists, faintly reminiscent of one of those small towns in the American mid-west with only a handful of staring people and little activity - to join the equally familiar S68, which would take us eastward through Volterra and on to pick up the *autostrada* at Poggibonsi. We really wanted to avoid major roads, but this one would give us a glimpse again of old Siena, this time in bright sunshine. (We had some thoughts of pausing there on our return journey.) The Menicaglis had suggested an overnight stay in Chianciano, a spa town which they visited themselves each year to refresh their livers. It was in the right direction, but just inside Tuscany still and we were hungry for Umbria. We also had unspoken concerns that it might be full of genteel elderly Italians, taking the waters. But we certainly planned a coffee stop there at least; they had been sending us postcards from Chianciano for years.

The driving went very well. We both find it easier to relax once we are safely back in Italy, and my wife's acute nervousness in the car happily abated. But progress was slow. We paused in Volterra, had lunch within sight of Siena, and stopped again late in the afternoon at Montepulciano (chiefly because of its lovely name); so that by the time we got to Chianciano it was really too late to consider going on to anywhere else for the night.

We were disappointed to find the tourist information office closed - and worried, too, for the town was indeed full of elderly well-to-do Italians (it was some kind of season for taking the cure) and accommodation might be at a premium. They were all expensively attired and strolling slowly up and down the main thoroughfare in a stately *passeggiata* of the aged - presumably filling the time between afternoon cure and dinner.

Addresses of hotels and other accommodation were displayed in the window of the information office, though without advice on vacancies. For a time it seemed the town did not have a single bed available; but with persistence (it was already starting to go dark so we had no other choice) we at last found an adequate *albergo* with a handy car park at the rear. I remember nothing more about the place except for a fellow guest at dinner. We noticed him the moment we entered the dining room; his face was extraordinarily familiar. It can be difficult to place someone when you see them in quite the wrong surroundings, but we were convinced we knew this man. He was unusual in that he was occupying a table alone (the others were rather crowded). We sat at a table for two just across the room from him, feeling half inclined to nod. But we couldn't be sure. Certainly he gave no sign of recognising us. The meal proceeded and we couldn't help looking his way from time to time. Who on earth could he be? Something about the fact that he was dining alone, with a grave expression on his face, seemed to offer a clue. But still his identity eluded us. Then, as we were leaving, we experienced a delicious mutual moment of realisation. The man was sitting in his proper place after all, for this was surely the food inspector from *Fawlty Towers*, on his holidays!

Next day we had to decide where exactly we wanted to visit in Umbria; so far it had been just a general idea. We quite liked the thought of staying close to water. Except in the north, Italy has few lakes of any size. We saw from the map that we happened to be quite near to two of the biggest: Trasimeno to the east of Chianciano (the only one actually in Umbria), and Bolsena to the south, near Orvieto. After so much driving the previous day, we settled on the closer Trasimeno. We planned to find a good hotel on its shores and settle there for a couple of days.

But what a disappointment it was: no sign of a hotel of *any* kind on its shores, nor any pretty villages dotted around the lake. Just emptiness. This might I suppose have had a grim connection with the massacres in the region back in Roman times, though that couldn't explain the flat and featureless landscape. And this was our first taste of Umbria! We drove on in silence, following the shoreline. It just wouldn't do. We could backtrack and head down to Bolsena, leaving Umbria, but would it be any more attractive? Pressing on, we began to see signs for Perugia. In the absence of an inviting stretch of water, why not go there? We hadn't till then given it much thought (I don't think the Menicaglis had ever been there); but it was Umbria's most important city, and the cities of Italy were our chief enthusiasm, if we reflected. Already it was mid-afternoon. Soon we would start to worry again about where to stay. You could always find *somewhere* reasonable in a city, and we were now quite close. It was the only choice.

Perugia turned out to be a vast medieval fortress-city (once an Etruscan stronghold), sprawled over a hilltop, with a busy modern town below - which of course we hit first. Reaching the historical part was easy on foot, via a number of ancient gates and other points of access; but more difficult by car. In fact it looked impossible at this stage. We drove in aimless frustration for a long time before hitting on the idea of temporarily abandoning the car and making the ascent on foot to look for accommodation. But then even finding a car park wasn't easy when you were being swept along. By the time we had got the thing off our hands and scrambled up the hill, the tourist information office (always our first port of call) was about to close. The lady suggested a couple of small hotels literally as she locked up for the night. Both, when we inspected them, looked to be pretty shabby, and so narrow were the streets that they lacked not only a car park proper but even a convenient place to pause for unloading. Not for the first time we reflected on the wisdom of the package tour. But we had to pick one of them. Darkness would soon be falling again.

Our choice reluctantly made, the next steps were to bring up the car, deposit our luggage in the hotel somehow in spite of the restricted access, return the car to the car park, then finally to climb the hill one more time on foot. My wife elected to wait in the hotel, unappetising as it was, and then to be ready to help with the unloading when I arrived. I had taken careful note of one access road (via a tunnel) on the way up, so the first part was relatively easy. We did have a brief, incoherent argument with a man next door, who seemed to be claiming that we were somehow infringing his civil rights; but it was only a minor distraction in the circumstances. We lugged our baggage up the musty staircase, and minutes later I was negotiating the awkward descent to dump the car again.

That proved to be the big problem. By now it was quite dark, and also the middle of Perugia's rush hour. The traffic picked me up and swept me along more helplessly than ever. The car park just wasn't there any more, and even if it had been I doubt that I would have been able to swing into it. Nor could I spot an alternative one. I was carried in circles for the best part of an hour, in what seemed like an increasingly bizarre dream sequence - just what the hell was I doing in the rush hour in Perugia? - until I happened to notice I was back at my starting point and realised it was time to return, defeated, to the hotel. My wife, meanwhile, had begun to panic, both about my long absence and the slightly creepy atmosphere of the hotel. When I explained about my failure to dump the car she wouldn't stay there a minute longer and insisted on joining me to have another go. This was a new worry, given her fear of heavy traffic; but in the event she calmly took on the role of looking out for a car park (the healing powers of Italy were working in mysterious ways) while I concentrated on the road. At last we found a 24-hour one, with a man on duty still who could explain the system. Now we had only to climb the hill one last time and find somewhere adequate for dinner, which was easy. We didn't bother to change, or even to wash.

That night we had little sleep. Convinced the bed was damp, we lay worrying about the moisture seeping into our bones. Confronting the odd couple running the place seemed unwise, and the only alternative was to sleep on the floor, which looked even less salubrious. Next morning we declined breakfast and walked out for what we thought would be a last look at old Perugia. But to our surprise in daylight we found we loved it. We breakfasted on the main square in the early morning sunshine, then paid the tourist office another visit.

The same lady was on duty, though now she was naturally in a far more helpful mood. And this time she had just the place for us. Much the best hotel in Perugia is the Brufani, on the Piazza Italia. She wasn't precisely directing us there, but she explained that within the Brufani was the separate but much less expensive Palace Hotel Bellavista. This was intriguing: how could the second hotel be a part of the first yet have a separate identity- and tariff? Her English was good, but we thought there must be some misunderstanding. We found, however, that the Brufani and the Bellavista were indeed one and yet separate. The cheaper hotel had its own less imposing entrance, but inside the marble halls and general facilities were largely shared, unless there was a demarcation line that the eye couldn't discern. I imagine the Brufani did have more luxurious rooms, but ours was excellent, even so, with marvellous views over the old-town rooftops to distant rolling hills. There was even a car park on the square - terribly congested, though the man explained that we would find a space easily enough when everyone had moved off for the day. This meant that we could take our time in retrieving the car and collecting our luggage from the other hotel.

Driving back up the hill, we found ourselves behind a big, old-fashioned car which we felt certain was British, though we couldn't quite place the model. Later, when we were ready to try to park, this car again appeared ahead of us, fighting for one of the scarce spaces. We could see a couple inside, the lady at the wheel and dealing somewhat imperiously with the situation while the man apparently slumbered beside her. Their car was quickly accommodated and they climbed out with some difficulty, the lady, in a large straw hat and expensive clothes, plainly still in charge. We saw now that they were quite ancient people, but carried along still by the confidence of wealth. They did not give the Bellavista entrance so much as a glance. Help was summoned from the Brufani and they were guided safely inside, masses of luggage quickly following. But then my wife really did surprise me. She told me she knew them, or at any rate the lady. They weren't characters from a television sitcom, either. In fact they were from the next village to ours and she had often met the lady in connection with her job. Later we found them standing at the balustrade at one end of the square, taking in the view, and had a little chat. I wanted to tell them that despite being no admirer of the wealthy, they struck me as a rather fabulous pair of ancients, out here unaccompanied in the wilds of Umbria. But of course that wouldn't do at all and I had to be content with a more mundane exchange of information.

You couldn't truthfully call Perugia beautiful; not seen from within. The main Piazza IV Novembre is a grey expanse surrounded by stone buildings which, despite much architectural detail, are impressive chiefly on account of their massive solidity. The great flanks of the Palazzo dei Priori and the Cattedrale di San Lorenzo could induce outdoor claustrophobia. There is no softness anywhere. Even the elaborately carved central Fonte Maggiore is protected by iron railings and could not be described as playful.

And yet we found something deeply appealing about the place. Perhaps the main attraction was the authenticity of the old city. This seemed like the very real Middle Ages, not some ersatz version; a place of hard certainty and harsh justice. You had a much stronger sense of discovery than is experienced in the more famous Italian cities - the illusion that you were among the first to see these things, rather than simply following in the footsteps of ten million previous tourists. Even the religious art - which of course you could hardly get away from - seemed to mean more in a purer context. Usually I grow tired pretty quickly of looking closely at cultural artifacts, preferring to dwell on the more general scene. Seldom do I leave a city with the feeling that I have missed some important object of veneration. But Perugia was different. We had only a few days there, which barely allowed time to scratch the surface. I regretted that we could not see more.

And nearby was Assisi, which also ate into our limited time. It would have been natural to drive there, but we were fearful of losing our cherished parking space prematurely. Instead, on our third morning, we took the by now familiar lighted passage down through the remains of the Rocca Paolina fortress to the new town and caught a train.

The line does not pass through Assisi itself; you are deposited a kilometre or two to the south and have to catch a bus. On the day of our visit there was a great crush and the buses were only every half hour or so. Everyone knew something about Saint Francis and so was trying to behave with appropriate dignity and patience; but on the other hand none of us wanted to risk missing the bus and having to wait another bloody half hour. The subtle jostling for position was thus very interesting to observe. You had to fix yourself rigidly to the spot while wearing an expression of gentle indifference to anything so mundane. And of course when the bus finally appeared a new tension took hold, so that you were trying now to maintain a kindly smile which barely concealed a snarl. It was something of a game of poker - though one which broke up with perhaps less goodwill than is customary. In fact it rapidly degenerated almost into a fight. We held our ground, however, and just managed to scramble aboard. Saint Francis himself would have had no chance.

That little skirmish, I am sorry to say, is my clearest memory of the excursion. We certainly wandered around the basilica and took photographs from a number of angles. Inside were to be seen a number of relics, including a tunic worn by the saint; his tomb; and frescoes by Giotto with their wicked eyes. The trouble was that, although an agnostic, I felt myself already in tune with Saint Francis' message of peace and kindliness, and wished the same could always have been said of the Christian Church itself. Afterwards we explored the streets of the small town and found a pleasant balcony restaurant for lunch, with hanging baskets still in full bloom.

Next morning, back in Perugia, we had breakfast outdoors again and wrote postcards at the table to send off before leaving. I took them to the post office while my wife did a bit of last minute exploring on her own. This turned out to be a huge place with several rooms - a converted palace, perhaps. I joined what seemed like the right queue, but when I finally reached the counter I was told that stamps had to be purchased elsewhere. I did my best to remonstrate, but lacked the necessary vocabulary and so was obliged to walk away with only a red face. I couldn't quite believe that they weren't able to sell you stamps at *any* damned counter position in a post office, but I took a good deal more care in choosing another queue, even so. I also watched the people in front, and was gratified to see that stamps were indeed being exchanged for money. At length only a small and very old Italian gentleman stood between me and the counter clerk. I had already been in the place for about twenty minutes, however, and so was by now on rather a short fuse.

The old man also had postcards in his hand, far more in fact than I was carrying. I heard very indistinct things being said, then the clerk passed across a number of stamps, mostly still in one sheet. Next the old man began laboriously to tear them off one by one and stick them to his cards. There was a certain amount of muttering, but no way would he be deflected from this. At last he reached the final card - but all the stamps were now used up!

He looked around him in some amazement, then across at the man behind the counter, as if to demand an explanation. The clerk was losing his cool. He said a number, very curtly. The old man looked under his cards, then down at the floor, then at people nearby, and finally back across the counter. The clerk was now silent. After a long pause, the old man very slowly reached deep into his trouser pocket and brought out a few coins. The clerk gave them a quick glance, then dismissed them for some reason with a wave of the hand. The old man dug deeper, but came up with nothing more. The clerk began to make shooing motions, while looking over the old man's head to attract the attention of the next person in the queue - myself. But still the old man would not budge. Instead, judging that I had had the best independent view of the transaction, he appealed to me for help - in incomprehensible Italian.

"*Non capisco!*" I said, in my well-practiced way. "*Sono inglese!*"

But he was as deaf to this as old Ivo had been back in Castellina years before, and babbled on. Suddenly I had had more than I could stand of having to cope with people who spoke a fundamentally different language. Something snapped.

"Look, you silly old fool," I said to him, as if he were a child, "there's absolutely no point in asking *me* for help, because the truth is that I can't understand a bloody word you're saying. I'm from England, you see. Across the water, beyond France, up in the wastes of northern Europe. We speak a different language up there. Ours is derived mainly from the Germanic languages, I understand, rather than Latin, though many of our words are from that source. Of course I did *do* Latin for a while at school, years ago. And French, too. In fact I've got an *O-level* in French. But not in *Italian*, you see, and that I'm afraid is the problem..."

Quite what - beyond accumulated frustration - impelled me to launch into this absurd John-Cleese style tirade, I'm not sure; but it did its job, for the man backed away, then turned and fled. A lady immediately behind had been listening with some curiosity. "I think you handled that very well," she said. She was Australian.

We bypassed Siena again on the journey back into Tuscany, heading instead for San Gimignano, where we hoped to spend the night. Alas, it was completely awash with tourists, so that we did well to find somewhere for a light lunch. The tourist information office, with no accommodation of their own to offer, were now doing business on behalf of neighbouring towns and found a room for us in Volterra.

Here again we had car problems - that seemed to be the main theme of this holiday. As with our first hotel in Perugia, access for cars was very difficult. But the hotel had reserved spaces on a communal car park at the edge of the town, some distance away. This the man attempted to explain when I passed through reception to attend to the car after dropping off my wife and our luggage. I had some difficulty grasping the gist of what he was saying, but at length he produced a crudely drawn street plan with the car park indicated by a cross. He was reluctant to lend it to me, however; I almost had to steal it from under his nose. And when I tried in the car to relate the streets of Volterra to this map, it didn't make much sense. But the town is quite small, and after a certain amount of circling I finally located a car park which I thought had to be the right one. Then I walked back to the hotel and found another crazy Englishman in reception, engaged in precisely the same difficult conversation. I slipped the street plan around his elbow and was about to leave when it struck me that I could be of assistance. The problem was that the man had his back to me and was listening intently to the instructions he was receiving. I coughed and said excuse me and tried other ways to engage his attention; but so absorbed was he in the effort to comprehend that he could only see me as an interfering nuisance. I even picked up the map again and waved it in front of his face, but even that failed to alert him to my offer of help. Perhaps my own mild derangement was too visible, I don't know. In the end I left him to it, deciding he must actually be enjoying the linguistic challenge. It was part of the fun of Italy, after all.

But from there the rest of this one-week holiday was downhill - literally and steeply so as we descended from Volterra's dramatic hilltop position to pick up the S68 once more, which follows the Cecina river through the Valle di Cecina, westward to the coast. We were scheduled to have dinner with the Menicaglis again on our final evening, and to sleep at the villa. Before that we planned to visit the coastal towns, then to spend the afternoon in Castellina itself. On the way we suddenly spied a quintessential Tuscan scene - rolling hills, bluer and paler as they receded; vineyards; cypresses; a solitary, single-track winding road; a cluster of sun-faded farm buildings out alone in a simultaneously green and parched landscape - which we simply had to photograph.

Cecina is quite large, with good shops; though we have never understood the mania to shop abroad when the money could be spent on better restaurants and hotels. Travelling north you cross the mouth of the river, and a little further on is Vada. This is a relatively insignificant town, which in our experience can nevertheless be mistaken for Cecina itself when travelling the other way. Soon after Vada you leave the pine-wooded shore and campsites to enter briefly an industrial area, after which is Castiglioncello. Although the season was over, there were a few holidaymakers about and the odd eating place, with a splash of coloured parasols, open for business; though you could see that Castiglioncello did not yet pose a threat to the Spanish costas. We had a pizza, wandered onto the beach (where I got into a argument with a dog, which for all we knew could have been rabid), clambered over the rocks (partly to escape), then decided to return to the car and drive up to Castellina without further delay. We hadn't had time to pause there on the day of our arrival, and now felt a sudden nostalgic hunger to wander its streets again.

We found the village changed, but only slightly. There were a few new villas, though not too many. The shops and other buildings in the centre looked a little brighter and better maintained, though scarcely garish. There was a new bypass road, but of only very modest scope. The small park, with its little pond with low surrounding wall which Rebecca had liked to walk on and had once fallen off into the water, had been beautified a bit, but still could not quite be described as beautiful. In short, the village remained unspoilt. Likewise the people. Sadly, old Ivo was no longer among them.

CHAPTER 7

LAKE GARDA - 1991

Our love affair with Italy continued in the summer of 1990 with a second brief visit to Venice - a repeat of our 1984 trip over the water from Rovinj, though this time the girls (on holiday with us but now semi-independent young women) declined to come along. The weather was extremely hot, limiting one's capacity to wander. In fact I am sorry to say that we sat in the shade in St Mark's Square for longer than was good for us, eating ice cream. To be in Venice again was wonderful, but to be there and not feel compelled to charge around was luxury indeed! We were only really confirming that Venice was the most beautiful city on earth, and that one day we simply must make the time to explore it with the love and attention it demanded. On this hot August afternoon we could barely stir ourselves; though I do recall a pleasant meal, followed by a leisurely gondola trip on the minor canals. Then it was time to return to Istria. (That happened only six years ago as I write, yet there was scarcely a hint in the news of the impending tragedy in Yugoslavia.)

The following year, restricted to the summer months but wearying a little of excessive heat, we decided for our last full family holiday to head for Lake Garda, where we believed the weather should be endurable. The Italian lakes were almost in the Alpine region, after all. You could picture mountain streams, perhaps still carrying traces of ice, emptying into them. The air would be pure, with just a hint of winter chill on the mild breeze. In other words, we would have the benefit of a giant outdoor air-conditioning system.

Maybe most summers that's the way it is up there, but 1991 was not one of those years. I think it must have been the hottest ten days we ever spent anywhere - hotter certainly than Venice, and hotter even than Sorrento. (Years before I had spent time in the West Indies and South America while serving in the Merchant Navy, and couldn't remember having experienced such heat even in those places.) But I am not being quite accurate. I mean that the temperatures *reached* on Lake Garda were the hottest we had known. What happened was that the heat built up steadily over a period until something had to happen or everyone would be baked alive. Then the pressure cooker was relieved at last by thunderstorms - sometimes highly dramatic ones, especially after dark when they crackled across and illuminated the lake. The cycle took about a week, the temperature after the storms dipping to a quite tolerable level so that you briefly considered perhaps donning a vest.

Actually, that's just how it was on the evening of our arrival. The storms had battered the town the night before. One consequence was that the lights of our hotel kept going out. This happened even as we stood waiting at reception, already having doubts about its suitability. Italian hotels can be surprisingly shabby. After our excellent accommodation in Yugoslavia the year before, we felt pretty let down. But in the end we managed not to complain, even when the lift also failed to work. I had grown up in the austerity years just after the war, and despite subsequent world travels could not help feeling that to be in such an exotic place at all was pretty amazing. I also hated the idea of being yet another whingeing English tourist, for I delight in seeing such people put firmly in their place. (Once on a return flight from Ibiza, delayed through no fault of the tired cabin staff, a particularly puffed-up male passenger had made such a fuss that the stewardess finally asked if he would like to complain personally to the captain on the flight deck. He disappeared through the little door wearing a smug expression; then re-emerged a moment later ashen-faced and totally silenced.)

How to compare the beauty of Venice, Sorrento (the panoramic view), a quintessential Tuscan landscape, and now Lake Garda? It would be foolish to try. Beauty is not only in the eye of the beholder, but also unquantifiable. So, a few facts instead:

Garda is reckoned to be the largest of the lakes, depending on how you do the measuring. Certainly it's the widest and has the greatest area. Roughly guitar-shaped, it points northwards into the Trentino Alto Adige region. It is farther from foreign borders than its principal rivals, Maggiore and Como, and is said to be more Italian, or less "Swissified". The nearest city is Verona, of Shakespeare and amphitheatre fame, only twenty-five kilometres from the southeast corner. The landscape around the broader southern end is relatively flat, becoming ever more dramatically scenic as you sail north. Our hotel was in Garda town, on the eastern shore at a point where the views begin to be truly glorious. Sailings by steamer or hydrofoil are readily available but quite expensive. You find yourself using them beyond the needs of travel or sightseeing in the hot weather, even so, since they represent the only practical alternative to immersing yourself permanently in your hotel pool for cooling off. The hydrofoils provide an especially effective spray-laden refreshing gale out on deck.

We found Garda to be not the most picturesque of the lakeside towns. There are some older buildings - villas and such, mostly fairly hidden - and narrow medieval lanes; though much of it is of comparatively recent construction, and consequently devoid of any real interest. We spent most time on the waterfront, where there are attractive promenade walks and numerous restaurants, often cooler inside than outdoors under a canopy. This is not a gastronomic memoir, but I must briefly mention the salmon-trout.

We were staying half-board at the hotel and ought to have been content with a light lunch each day. We soon drifted into the habit of a more substantial midday repast, however, with salmon-trout a prime choice on the menu, washed down with white wine and mineral water. The fish were said to be directly from the lake, though you did wonder about fish-farms. They were perfectly delicious, even so. This was also a good time to study the waiters at work. Head waiters in even quite modest restaurants in Italy seem to possess still an almost military authority over their underlings, and to delight in having this power fully on display. Besides barking orders and generally bristling, they play little games with the lower ranks, who are usually bursting with frustration, both because they are apt to be much younger and hence able to understand that the strutting boss is likely to be a deeply unsympathetic figure in the eyes of many foreign visitors, and also because they take great pride in their table skills and resent being denied opportunities to flourish them. Sometimes the tension, as the hovering head waiter made as if to assist with some table need, then drew back, then muscled in once more at a sensitive moment, could render you unappreciative of the fine skill with which the bone could be taken from the fish or a wine glass expertly replenished, and ultimately put you off the salmon-trout altogether.

We had one particularly bad experience of that kind on a visit to Sirmione, I recall. The head waiter's performance was so outrageous, and the suffering of his subordinate so palpable, that we came very close to walking out. But then we thought that might be playing into the head waiter's hands, for he clearly had the authority to blame anything and everything on his staff if he so desired.

Business was less than brisk, too, and you could believe that to be deemed responsible for a customer walk out might be tantamount to asking for the sack. So we sat it out. The meal itself was quite wonderful, but on a subsequent visit to the town we couldn't face the strain and embarrassment again so we dined elsewhere.

Sirmione is situated right at the southern end of the lake, on an extraordinarily slender little peninsula no more than a hundred metres wide at its narrowest point. We had rather avoided it on our first boat excursions because of its poor landscape setting, but it turned out to be the most visually striking town on Garda, and to command wide and lovely views to the mountains in the north - though this would depend on where you were in the weather cycle. After the storms the views across the lake would be crystal clear, but as the temperature rose a mistiness developed. Fortunately the visibility was good on both of our visits. The medieval centre of Sirmione is dominated by the fairytale Castello Scaligera, which you could take for a nineteenth-century folly, so perfectly preserved and comparatively unweathered are its towers and battlements, but is evidently the real thing - genuine thirteenth-century. I suppose it hasn't seen much military action.

Our very first boat trip was to Riva, at the extreme northern end of the lake. The town faces the sun, so that flowers and other vegetation grow luxuriantly, as elsewhere on Garda; but up there the mountains seem to press in on you in an uncomfortable way. We weren't inclined to stay for very long. For those with a less developed sense of outdoor claustrophobia there are a few things to see in Riva, such as the old castle, the Rocca, which houses a civic museum, and the church of the Inviolata. Water sports - yachting and windsurfing - flourish up in the north on account of the strong and unusual winds. They can be viewed at close hand as you sail south once more. The winds cause rather more capsizing than you might normally expect to see, especially among the windsurfers, who as they struggle pathetically to right their shambolic craft seem unappreciative of their temporary respite from the burning heat.

The ferries crisscross the lake, so the first stop going south might be Torbole, on the eastern side, followed by Limone, on the west. Pedants insist that the name Limone derives not from the fruit but from the Latin word for frontier, *limen* - though you would think of a frontier as a line (the lake shore, perhaps) rather than one spot. The town has ancient lemon groves, too! It's an exquisite place. It is also described here and there as *lively* and may become so after dark, though we were thankfully there only in the afternoon. Further south, on the eastern shore again, is Malcesine, which has perhaps the best position of all the lakeside towns, and magnificent views across the water. With its small harbour and romantically situated castle, it is equally picturesque for the near-sighted. We took the cable-car up to the Bocca Tratto Spino - an experience that was at once agreeable and disconcerting. In only a few minutes you were transported into a much cooler, more northerly climate. It seemed quite uncanny, almost magical.

Fair Verona I remember only through a heat-haze. We went twice: on the second hottest day of our holiday; and then again on the very hottest, just before the storms, though that was an evening visit. Our first excursion was by train. By late morning the temperature was already in the mid-thirties and still climbing. In the hottest places in Italy they seem to delight in displaying the temperature in public squares. We were loitering listlessly near the amphitheatre, wondering how best to set about exploring the city without exposing ourselves to heatstroke or skin cancer, when we noticed a sign advertising a bus tour. Normally we might have disdained such an idea, but on this day it seemed like a Godsend. (On a trip to Russia two or three years before guides had been unavoidable, but also fascinatingly candid, since *glasnost* was just getting into its stride - maybe that helped change our attitude.)

The bus turned out to be a very small minibus. At first we thought it would be driver only, but there was an unexplained delay and then a surprisingly young girl came running around the corner, slightly dishevelled and a little flustered, as though she had been called to do the job at the very last moment, as may indeed have been the case. There were only six or seven passengers, but when she enquired a show of hands revealed that we spoke four languages between us. This was naturally a problem; though not as it turned out a linguistic one, for she proved to be remarkably fluent in all of them. The difficulty was cramming in four commentaries as we moved at some speed through the streets. Important buildings, monuments and places of historical and cultural interest swept past (Verona is renowned for its pink-hued old palaces and villas), all fully described for the benefit of everyone on board at astonishing speed by our young guide, without noticeable pause for breath. It reminded me of a television film I had once seen about Einstein's daily tram journeys to the Patent Office as a young man. As the tram speeded up the passing buildings seemed to become thinner, and that set him to thinking about relativity. On our rapid bus tour of the sights of Verona something weird happened instead to the speed of sound. At first it was intolerable, and made more so because our guide was equipped for some unfathomable reason with a microphone when she was no more than an arm's length from anyone. What with the different languages and the deafening delivery, the information she was so skilfully communicating went largely unheeded. But then we gradually got used to it, and were able to relax. I can remember next to nothing of what we saw, however. We certainly paused at an elevated spot to take in a panoramic view of the city through the shimmering heat-haze, the Adige River snaking through its heart. And we inevitably visited the little square with its balcony and charming statue of *Giulietta*. Curiously, she was down at ground level rather than on her balcony, having evidently given up her plaintive appeals from on high in favour of a more direct search for the elusive Romeo (who still hadn't showed).

Our second visit, as might be expected, was to the amphitheatre. No one can be in the vicinity of Verona without feeling a powerful urge to go to the opera, no matter how weak their actual interest in opera as such. It seems such a glamorous thing to do, and everyone is sure to be deeply envious back home. Nothing but pleasure is anticipated. How could anyone fail to be absolutely thrilled by witnessing one of the great classics of this most sumptuous of art forms in such a setting? Just take along your chilled wine and picnic hamper, then lie back and immerse yourself in the sheer magnificence of it all!

Well, perhaps our mistake was to settle for the least expensive tickets. But while our seats were to be way up in the Roman equivalent of the "gods", we convinced ourselves it should be as good a place as any in an arena said to have perfect acoustics. We thought there was a chance we might have the best view, too.

Our opera ordeal began at five-thirty in the afternoon. We missed dinner, but imagined there might be an opportunity to eat somewhere en route - or at least to buy drinks (perhaps even chilled wine), though we did have a plentiful supply of bottled water with us (as advised). It was a long, slow drive by coach in stifling heat, but our minder reassured us that there was plenty of time as we only had to be at the amphitheatre by seven-thirty. She warned, however, that there would be a tremendous crush and that we must on no account lose contact with her - particularly *after* the show, if we wanted to avoid being left behind. A group dash to the coach would be necessary to avoid the post-opera gridlock. On the way, depending on time, parking difficulties and other factors such as pavement congestion, it might just be possible to buy refreshments from a shop she had in mind. As for use of the toilet, she hoped we had all dealt with that before leaving as opportunities might be difficult, or more likely nonexistent, from now on.

We did manage against the odds to buy a few cans of coke, plus crisps and such; then we joined the crush of opera supporters outside the arena. It was like an impatient, angry football crowd, all elbows and toe-treading. But once through the barrier things became a little easier and we were able to buy a programme and seat cushions. These latter were again as advised, though as it turned out they were more needed for insulation than for comfort, for the stone seating proved to be almost too hot to touch, even so late in the day. (Later we heard that the temperature in the arena that day had touched forty degrees.) From the outside the walls do not look to be very high, so that you would expect the inside depth also to be modest. When we at last reached our high seats and looked down, however, we saw that the stage and arena floor were an incredible distance away - seemingly far below the outside ground level. We had also imagined that seated on terraces we would have leg room and a back rest. In the event we found ourselves having to sit bolt upright to avoid touching the legs of the person in the row behind, while to the front we had to watch our feet to avoid kicking someone's back. As for elbow room, there was none. Reaching a trouser pocket involved rotating the trunk through ninety degrees, and then you risked interfering with the legs to the rear. We were seated well before eight and feeling thoroughly uncomfortable in only a matter of minutes. Upon managing the necessary contortions to open the programme, we learned that the opera was to begin at nine-thirty!

Our drinks and snacks were soon consumed, leaving only the water bottles, which instinct told us ought to be held in reserve. Instead we began to try to summon one of the refreshment vendors. These tray-carrying young men were extraordinarily agile and sure-footed. Where any normal person would soon have stumbled and crashed down among the bodies, they were able nimbly to stride about the arena on their unnaturally long legs, finding tiny foot spaces between the thighs and knees, their heads meanwhile twisting energetically this way and that as they scanned the sea of faces for business. The preparations down on stage being too distant to watch, these mountain goats of the terraces were the only available entertainment as we waited for the main event - at least until it began to go dark. But we never did succeed in buying anything from them.

And so at long last to the opera itself. We saw the tiny figures appear below and take up what seemed to be their starting positions; then we noticed that the performance had evidently begun. But where were the rich sounds of the orchestra and the powerful voices of the singers? Something was wrong. The music reaching us was so faint that you wondered if you were hearing it at all. Did they have microphones? Was there an electrical fault somewhere? One's first instinct was to search for the volume control button, but these were not provided. Then, as the time began to pass, it dawned on us that this was all the volume we were likely to get. It was as though we were in not so much another room as another town.

Nor were things much better visually. We were watching side on to begin with, and everything was all so distant - not to mention the fact that it was by now fully dark. We gathered from the reactions of the well-to-do people in the expensive seats at floor level that spectacular things were happening on stage, but they were largely lost on us. The performance seemed mainly to consist of a series of grand entrances and set-pieces rather than to follow a coherent story line. Certain arias were I'm sure repeated simply because they were favourites with the audience. The best thing about it was that it was all in Italian. I don't like to read or hear the English translated version at the best of times.

Midnight passed and they were still playing the encores, while we remained trapped on our stone seats, which even now were very warm to the touch. We still had most of our water, too. By the time we had thought to drink the stuff the bottles were as warm as the stones. But we had long ago given up worrying about touching the legs to our rear and the backs facing us. Everyone had become more friendly in that respect. When the final whistle - or last encore - came we somehow sprang to our feet and chased for the exit, not daring to break our stride until we had clambered aboard the coach once more. Now there only remained the forty kilometre drive through the night to Garda. By half-past-one we were tucked up in bed. No one, thankfully, had felt the need to use the toilet all evening. In fact we must have been close to severe dehydration.

Oh yes - the opera? It was *Rigoletto*, I believe. At any rate someone kept breaking faintly into "La Donna è Mobile" from time to time.

CHAPTER 8

FLORENCE - 1992

This was my fourth visit to the city (if anyone is counting, we had an uneventful rainy-day excursion by train from Rosignano in 1980, which I haven't recorded). In 1992 my wife and I were there for a few days in February to celebrate an important wedding anniversary. The place was becoming familiar. I won't say we *belonged* there, but we certainly knew our way around. It's surprising how little time you need in a city to acquire that sense of familiarity. I recently watched the film of EM Forster's *A Room with a View*, and though it was photographed to give the appearance of a different age, most of the time I knew what was just around the corner or across the square. Florence looked beautiful, too, especially glimpsed through trees from the surrounding hills. It was presented as a very romantic place, and that was our feeling on this latest visit; though I have to say that something of my very first (1978) rather negative impression remained in my mind. Well, not long ago I picked up Mary McCarthy's book *The Stones of Florence*, expecting the usual paean to a much-loved city, and was surprised - even shocked - to find her taking a distinctly unromantic view of this birthplace of the Renaissance.

She was writing in the 1950s, since when things must have changed a little. Her particular *bête noire* is the motor scooter, and *they* have certainly become less common. She is also (in her introductory opening chapter) complaining mostly about the months of high summer, when the tourists are at their most dense (possibly in both senses). The closest I have been to that is May. But hers is no superficial whinge about the appalling heat and the hordes of uncomprehending foreign visitors: she also displays a quite profound dislike of modern Florence in all seasons - which, considering the amount of time she must have had to spend in the city researching the book, is somewhat strange. She wonders how the transient visitor can bear the place - not just the noise, the traffic and the heat, but something else besides: the fact that Florence seems dull, and provincial. "In the lacklustre cafés of the dreary main *piazza* (which has a parking lot in the middle)" - this is the celebrated Piazza della Signoria! - "stout women in sensible clothing sit drinking tea, and old gentlemen with canes are reading newspapers... Along the Arno, near Ponte Vecchio, ugly new buildings show where the German bombs fell." She describes it as a *manly* town, which makes no concession to the pleasure principle, standing foursquare and direct, with no air of mystery. Florentine palaces "bristle like fortresses or dungeons, their thick walls and bossy surfaces seem to repel the very notion of hospitality". The Piazza della Repubblica, with its triumphal arch, is "the ugliest in all Italy - a folly of nationalist grandeur committed at a time when Florence was briefly the capital of the new Italy".

This is simply not the sort of stuff that one expects to read about such a cultural Mecca; not at all the kind of thing one finds in the guidebooks and holiday brochures. What she is relentlessly determined to do is to correct the "false idea of Florence that grew up in the nineteenth century, thanks in great part to the Brownings and their readers - a tooled-leather idea of Florence as a dear bit of the old world". The city can never have been that at any time in its existence, she tells us. "History for Florence is neither a legend nor eternity, but a massive weight of rough building stone demanding continual repairs, pressing on the modern city like a debt, blocking progress."

The Stones of Florence is certainly an eye-opener. Having read it, you couldn't fail to view the city in a more knowing and cynical light. But I'm not sure I'm altogether in favour of having one's eyes opened - not *too* wide, anyway. There is something to be said for remaining unenlightened. It certainly aids the appreciation of visual delights. There can be too much of this ripping away of facades and kicking over of stones. I am glad I had yet to read Ms McCarthy's book in February 1992, and that I got to Florence for a fourth time still in a state of relative (and blissful) ignorance.

Our hotel - the Brunelleschi - just around the corner from the *duomo*, was more interesting than most. It was largely modern, but built around and integrated with a sixth-century Byzantine tower - the former Torre Pagliazza in the Piazza di Santa Elisabetta - the old stonework of which protruded here and there into the dining room and other areas. It was surprising to find a modern development of any kind right in the heart of the city. The cathedral dome, ingeniously designed and constructed by Brunelleschi (the man and architect) in the fifteenth century, appeared close at hand from certain windows. We settled there for what we felt sure would be a carefree few days, although in truth my wife had been feeling under the weather - caused, we believed, by a fast and unpleasant coach transfer from Pisa. In the middle of the visit we were considering a train trip down to Rosignano to see the Menicaglis.

The weather was fine and quite cool - much the best kind for exploring old Florence. On our first morning we witnessed some kind of trade union protest or procession, and even *that* seemed romantic. Bizarre, too. I'm sure the men had their legitimate grievances, but you couldn't help feeling that, living in Florence, what *more* could they want? Most of the famous sights we had of course seen on previous visits, but it can be very pleasant to renew your acquaintance with a city. Indeed, like love and music, places can be lovelier the second (or even third) time around. Unenlightened as yet by Mary McCarthy, we wandered the streets and squares, looked in the famous buildings, and poked about in the street markets, feeling it was all pretty wonderful. With the crush of tourists in February being quite light, we were able for the first time during our wanderings to spend as long as we wished inspecting the golden panels of Ghiberti's "Gate of Paradise" Baptistry door, and to get as close as we liked to the Fountain of the Wild Boar in the New Market. We also saw at last the original of Michelangelo's David in the Academy of Fine Arts. And at the end of the day, because we had booked only bed-and-breakfast at the Brunelleschi, there was the pleasure still to come of dining at a restaurant of our own choice.

On that second evening my wife still felt unwell - rather worse, in fact - though it seemed nothing much to worry about. We had a table reserved at a very inviting place just up from the Ponte Vecchio, and she was determined not to cry off. In fact we left the hotel early to stroll across the Piazza della Signoria by night and to walk down by the Arno; then we headed for our chosen dining place. The head waiter on this occasion was tall, distinguished-looking and gracious, and not in the least inclined to lord it over his subordinates. The place was busy without being *too* busy, a balance which is rarely achieved (too often in a restaurant you are either almost alone, or else conscious of the encroachment of other diners). And the service, too, was neither too fast nor too slow, but just right. In short, on a romantic evening in Florence, everything seemed as good as you could wish. After a glass or two of wine the conversation began to flow nicely; or at least I started to get into my stride, in characteristic fashion. But my wife was rather quiet now, I couldn't help noticing; even subdued. Then - somewhere in the main course - she said she was going to faint.

And without further ado that is precisely what she did, in quite spectacular fashion, falling backwards off her chair and ending up in an undignified heap close to a wall. At first I just couldn't believe what had happened. It was quite unprecedented; she had no history whatever of this kind of thing. Then, feeling equally full of concern and my own inadequacy (if ever my limited Italian was going to be put to the test this surely was the time!), I quickly got down and did my best to check she was unhurt and in no danger, rearranged her clothing, got her into the first-aid recovery position, and at the same time shouted orders in two languages to whoever would listen. Had I had to rely on the help of my fellow diners, things would have been truly desperate; but by great good fortune this happened to be an establishment fully equipped and trained to deal efficiently and sensitively with just such an occurrence. Their emergency procedure went smoothly into action. As I attended to my wife, who was beginning to come round, I was aware of tables being hastily repositioned, other diners being reassured, and then a side window being somehow drawn back for access when more expert help arrived. The head waiter meanwhile had retained his suave and unflappable manner. He spoke excellent English, explaining in a quiet voice that everything was fully under control and not to worry. Then a stretcher appeared, the patient was carried carefully out to the ambulance - and off we sped, blue light flashing, into the blackness of the ancient streets.

By the time we reached the hospital, having been shaken about a fair bit, my wife was feeling rather worse; but the whole business *was* beginning to seem over-dramatised. Whatever had caused the fainting - something she'd eaten, we now naturally assumed - she would have preferred to be taken by taxi back to the hotel. But of course we were now in the system. She was consigned to a bed and various routine tests were carried out. The immediate discovery was that her blood pressure was too high (for which she was given an injection). In fact she did have something of a history of high blood pressure, so to us it seemed relatively trivial. But when we tried to explain this to the medical staff they wouldn't listen. High blood pressure became what was wrong with her - the *only* thing. They didn't seem much interested any longer in the fainting. Soon we could tell that she was only going to be released when her blood pressure had returned to normal, and that of course was unlikely to happen, at least in the short term. We were at an impasse, which wasn't much helped by the language difficulty. English had been spoken in the ambulance, which as we had understood it was manned by volunteers; but in the hospital, presumably staffed by professionals, it seemed to be Italian or nothing. This was proving in some ways to be our lucky night, however, for we then caught the sound of an *American* voice from an adjoining room. It turned out to belong to a priest, or at any rate a churchman of some kind (he was dressed in jeans and a sloppy sweater), who by another amazing chance spoke fluent Italian. He was in Florence with some students, one of whom had needed minor hospital attention. They had been about to leave, but he was summoned in the nick of time and very kindly stood in as our interpreter. Even then it was only with the greatest reluctance (we were beginning to consider bribes) that the necessary forms were produced for signing and my wife at last released. The stress of the threatened open-ended confinement had almost caused a relapse, but one of the staff summoned a taxi for us and the final parting was very amicable. I have no idea who paid the bill.

We thought the crisis might be over, but next morning she felt groggy once more. That day we lounged about in the hotel for the most part, only venturing out for slow and unambitious strolls in the immediate neighbourhood. It was then that we discovered how unkind Florence can be to anyone in need of a sit down. There seemed to be no public seats anywhere on the streets, or even in the squares; and precious few green areas where you might have a stronger hope of finding the equivalent of a park bench. Our next thought was to stop for coffee somewhere, just to have the chance to sit for awhile. You found, though, that the Florentines like to take their coffee standing up. They don't use the refreshment ritual as we do, partly for physical recuperation from the exertions of the day. Aside from their digestions (very sensitive, I understand), you do wonder why they bother with coffee at all, since they appear invariably to order only *espresso*, in a tiny cup. I think in the end we resorted to the churches, though even there on certain days the seating seems mysteriously to have been spirited away.

The following day my wife was feeling much better again, so we decided to get out of Florence and take the train down to Rosignano, as planned. At least we would be guaranteed a long sit down. That thought of course invited a crowded train with no seats available, but in the event we watched the Tuscan towns and countryside go by in comfort and comparative solitude. Brenda was waiting for us as arranged at Rosignano, and after we had hinted at a nice further sit down for a *cappuccino* in a pleasant little supermarket café, off we drove up the familiar roads to dear old Castellina Marittima once more. We were surprised to see the ugly concrete supports for a new *autostrada* marching across the intervening landscape, but after recent events we weren't in the mood to feel excessively concerned about that. Otherwise things seemed unchanged since 1989, as might be expected. Roberto was able to leave work early and to join us for the late afternoon and evening. When we told them about the hospital experience, they seemed surprised that things had gone as smoothly and competently as they had. We got the impression that time in hospital for the natives could be a decidedly chancy affair. In some parts, we gathered, it could be necessary to install a permanent family presence at the bedside in order to ensure prompt and adequate treatment. It was a short and uneventful visit, but very pleasant for all that. We left them sadly with a wave at Rosignano station and haven't been back to Castellina since; though we fully intend to return, and for a longer stay again, before they finally decide to sell the villa (as has been hinted).

The Castellina excursion was a mysterious but happy respite from my wife's illness. Next morning - our final day - she was much worse. She felt quite unable to face the return coach trip to Pisa, so we ordered a taxi to take us to the station, with the intention of making our own way to the airport. That day was much the hardest to get through. We spent a fair part of it lying on the grass in the Boboli Gardens. I had wanted to see a Caravaggio exhibition in the Pitti Palace, but that couldn't be managed. There was one incident worth mentioning, however, as we were making our way back to the hotel for the last time. Since the night of the fainting, we had rather avoided the street where the restaurant was, partly for the ridiculous reason that we hadn't actually paid for our meal. But now we carelessly passed close by - and a moment later noticed the tall header waiter walking on the other side of road. We were quick to avert our faces, but he spotted us, and to our alarm began rapidly to cross in our direction. Could he *really* expect payment? We could hardly believe it possible. He loomed over us menacingly, so that it took a few moments for us to realise he was actually smiling and wanted only to express his relief and great pleasure that my wife was now apparently much recovered. He hoped she was enjoying the rest of her visit, and asked us to be sure to come to his restaurant again when we were next in Florence.

We were back resting in the Brunelleschi long before the taxi was due. It was a late flight, and the whole return journey a considerable ordeal. Back home, my wife immediately took to her bed. Only several days later, when she had begun to turn yellowish, did I have the sense at last to send for the doctor, who diagnosed either glandular fever or hepatitis - both highly debilitating illnesses, treatable only by rest and diet. We never did find out which it was.

CHAPTER 9

LAKE MAGGIORE - 1993

You might think that after some of these experiences - the Florence one in particular - we would have had enough of the country; but we were back in Italy fifteen months later, this time to mark a special birthday, visiting the Lakes again. Since then we have returned to Sorrento, and as I write (late summer 1996) have a two-week trip to Sicily coming up. So the visits are tending to become more frequent. No matter what happens there, it seems we never tire of the place. We haven't altogether neglected the rest of the world in the years since our first bold expedition to Tuscany in the late seventies, but there is nowhere else that we have visited twice, America (and Istria) aside. Italy, it has to be said, has become an obsession with us - *became* one, in fact, some years ago. We are, I think, well through the stage of boring people to death on the subject (at least in conversation!). And I don't believe we have ever consciously been tourist snobs; even if taking one's holidays there *is* becoming ever more fashionable nowadays among the rich and celebrated. The truth is that we now rather avoid encouraging friends and acquaintances to visit the country, and don't much mind if they don't; for we are content to have Italy as a place of special and deepening meaning in our own lives.

Lake Maggiore is much closer to the high mountains than Garda, with its top end actually in Switzerland. The climate is therefore reckoned to be more volatile. We saw something of this during our visit, though in general the weather remained relatively calm - and cool, since the month was only May. Our hotel was situated on the northern shore of Bay of Pallanzo, an offshoot that juts out to the west about a third of the way up the lake. At first we imagined this area, beautiful as it seemed, must be something of a backwater. Only later did we come to appreciate that we were at just about the finest spot on the entire shoreline. From our window on a clear day we could see the distant, snowcapped peak of

Monte Rosa, more than four-thousand six-hundred metres high, and closer at hand, just across the water, the exquisite little Borromean Islands, the prized gems of the western shore.

We had the kind of accommodation arrangement which we have sometimes enjoyed elsewhere: a room in a small, quiet hotel, with the freedom to use the more lavish facilities of a bigger one just up the road. This meant we could expect to sleep peacefully, and also to dine in some style, taking or leaving the in-house entertainment as we wished. In fact, as so often happens, dinner and the behaviour of the waiters, working and supervisory, soon became the evening's principal, if occasionally infuriating, diversion.

The cream-jacketed head waiter of the larger establishment was one of those *square* individuals you sometimes find yourself stuck behind at the cinema or on a crowded pavement - square in the geometric rather than non-trendy sense. He had a small head, pushed well down into his shoulders, which were wide, sharp-cornered and sloped upwards from the neck. His back view is imprinted on my memory, for that was what we had to look at through dinner most evenings. He liked to stand close to our table, sometimes even propping himself against it, as he directed operations.

Most of the time command was exercised by managerial telepathy, but he could be counted on to leave his mark at intervals and charge across the room to berate an underling. This happened when he spied new arrivals in the restaurant who were not in his judgment being welcomed and seated with proper obsequiousness. Then, often walking backwards, he would return slowly to and lean absently against our table, lost in a glow of supervisory satisfaction. He also used to circulate early in the meal, asking what was required from the dinner menu for the next evening and filling in chits. These he tended to slam down on the nearest table (usually ours) when the urge to intervene across the room suddenly took possession of him. Later, he wasn't always sure what he had done with the chits, and for a few moments might even look slightly nonplussed. The after-dinner lounge pianist, though unaccomplished, couldn't compete.

The Borromean Islands, named after a seventeenth-century count and local bigwig, and still owned by his descendants, are Isola Bella, Isola Madre and Isola Pescatori. (A fourth, San Giovanni, just off the shore at Pallanza, has a villa once owned by Toscanini, but is private.) With the entire mainland at the disposal of tourists, it does seem curious that everyone should want to sail out to and stroll around these tiny bits of land simply because they are surrounded by water, but one can't help but join them. In fact we spent little time on the two larger islands, Isola Madre especially, chiefly because of the crowds. Count Carlo III lavished most money and attention on Isola Bella, to create an elaborate garden with terraces for his wife; later adding a palace containing what are said to be very inferior works of art, though we didn't go in. One does wonder if the wife was altogether pleased with her island gift. Was she to be confined there? Did it become her prison? If the inferior works of art sometimes drove her outdoors and into the company of the white peacocks (also specially introduced at some point), she could not in those days have occupied herself trying to photograph them in the display mode, as most visitors were doing on the morning we were there, myself included. Why I'm not sure, since they are much less impressive than the more common species.

The slightly larger Isola Madre I remember less well, and it is possible that we may not have actually stepped ashore there. But I haven't forgotten and will never forget the smallest of these jewels of Lake Maggiore, Isola Pescatori, or Fishermen's Island.

I must say, though, that the concept of a fishermen's island struck me immediately as rather odd. Why would fishermen choose to make an *island* their base, especially such a very small one. It would be something like being confined still to a boat, when you might think that after a hard day on the water they would want to stretch their legs and relax with a wider range of people than just their fishing mates. But this again could have something to do with the powerful

Borromeo family, who apparently control all fishing rights on Maggiore even today. Maybe living on Pescatori was a condition for having access to the fishing grounds. This family does seem to have had a taste for forcing people to live on its islands. One inevitably wonders also about Isola Madre, and Count Carlo's mother.

Isola Pescatori is a very congested little place, though one end - the pointed end (it is even *shaped* something like a boat) - is occupied only by a curious avenue of stumpy trees, terminating at the point itself. They seem to have no purpose, unless they lead to the spot where the islanders ceremonially cast the bodies of their dead to the waves. The island can be crossed in half a minute, yet you can feel momentarily lost in its narrow cobbled alleyways (there are of course no real roads or motor traffic). Beached fishing boats can be seen around the shore, together with other evidence of fishing activity; but the main business nowadays must surely be tourism. Certainly the shops all cater pretty well exclusively for the visitors who arrive in small numbers with each ferry. We found this somehow acceptable, where elsewhere it can often seem intolerable. The general impression is of a freshly-painted little village with a tightly-packed assemblage of terracotta roofs. But Pescatori has been continuously inhabited since pre-Roman times, and there are genuine islanders living there today. It has a fine church, with a long history and a wealth of religious art and artifacts, besides of course a few hotels and restaurants. We timed our visit deliberately so as to have a fish lunch there and dined outdoors with a typical though hardly boring view back across the lake to Pallanza and the mountains beyond. To our surprise the establishment was run by another of those intrepid English ladies abroad. She told us she lived on the island right through the tourist season, but then had to leave when the sometimes stormy weather arrived later in the year. We imagined she retreated only to the mainland, but she explained that she went all the way home to England each winter. I'm pretty sure she said she'd been doing it since the forties. A curious life!

Because in May there was little need to cool off, we spent less time on the lake than we had on Garda two years before. One trip we had to make, though, was up to the extreme northern end. Sadly, it was a disappointment. Our natural assumption was that as you sailed north, up into Switzerland and deeper into the Alps, the mountains would become higher, the lake shore more rugged and the scenery ever more spectacular. In fact the opposite happens: you leave behind the best scenery and sail into a relatively flat and uninspiring region that seems hardly worth the price of the ticket. The snowcapped mountains are so distant as to be scarcely in view at all. Of course this is easily understood if you look at a relief map, but no one would think of doing that beforehand, except maybe mountain climbers. There were stops at the Swiss towns of Brissago, Ascona and finally Locarno, where we stepped ashore at last. It was hardly worth the bother. The lakeside promenade was quite pretty, but I think we were there on a Sunday. At any rate the place was scarcely bustling. We tried to exchange some Italian currency, and that led to an protracted dispute over the rate, after which we had already had enough. We didn't even try to eat there, but returned to the landing stage and caught the next ferry back into our beloved Italy.

A more satisfying *land* excursion was westwards to Macugnaga, a long climb following the Toce river and the Valle Anzasca. The road was every bit as hair-raising as the one to Amalfi. I am invariably tempted on such drives (always against my wife's wise advice) to perform contortions in taking photographs from the coach window so as to capture the drama outside. As ever the results were a great disappointment. Still photographs just don't do it. Macugnaga is a place of log cabins and Swiss-style chalets just below the snow line and in the shadow of Monte Rosa, existing chiefly for climbers, I imagine, though catering also for tourists of the more general kind. There was a perfect meadow just beyond the village. We had it to ourselves and were able to pick Alpine flowers for later pressing, and to re-enact for the benefit of our primitive camera mountain scenes from *The Sound of Music*. These turned out very well. After that we took the cable-car way up above the snow line to a point where we were promised spectacular Alpine views. Alas a thick mist came down even as we ascended, so that we might as well have been suffering from snow blindness. In fact it was so dense that we could barely manage an impromptu snowball fight. Our upward plunge into this severely wintry region was actually less of a shock to the system than the Malcesine experience on Garda two years earlier because we were entirely ready for it. We had even brought extra clothes.

For our major excursion of the holiday we decided to go into Milan in search of The Last Supper, taking an early ferry across the bay and picking up the train at Stresa. There was the usual *"due biglietti, andata e ritorno, per Milano Stazione Centrale"* at the ticket office, which my wife usually deals with as I find it a struggle. Not that I didn't know the words; the truth is that I often become quickly enmeshed in misunderstandings of some sort even when dealing with people across counters or through little windows in England. If someone else is available I am willing to stand back. (I remember the very first time I entered a bank to open an account the man behind the glass immediately threw me by asking, "What for?" It took about ten minutes for me to establish that he needed to know if I wanted a current or deposit account. Before that point was reached I had made a long speech in defence of basic freedoms.) The journey into the city was uneventful, reinforcing our smug belief that travelling in Italy was simplicity itself when you knew what you were doing. (This foolish complacency would not survive the return journey later in the day.)

Milan is a busy centre of commerce, less oriented towards the tourist than Italy's other major cities; but there is still a great deal more to see of the cultural and historical kind than can possibly be encompassed in just a few hours. Moreover, the visitor is unlikely to be as familiar in advance with the principal landmarks and points of interest as, say, in Venice or Rome. So, as a day-tripper in Milan, the only sensible approach is to seek out the places that you know can't be missed, hoping for a few chance discoveries along the way.

Tourists who have a camera on their shoulder and their nose forever in a map are much ridiculed, besides offering themselves as easy targets for petty thieves; yet I have never found a way of negotiating a large city purely by instinct. My wife fixes her compass by the main roads, which after a while turn into *the* main road. If we take care not to lose our bearings in relation to *that*, she thinks no further aids to navigation are needed. I won't say that one method has proved more successful than the other. Like most couples, I fancy, we find our way around by an occasionally inflammable mixture of science and sixth sense. From the station, for instance, we strolled only a short distance down the Via Pisani before we were faced with a choice of at least six different directions. I immediately paused to dig deep into our flight bag for the street plan I had taken care to bring along, while she merely tested the general ambience with her sensitive nose and set off in what she knew was the right direction for the opera house and the cathedral.

And she was right. Very soon, without even trying, we were in the Piazza della Scala. In the middle of the square was our first chance discovery, a statue of Leonardo. Unfortunately it was on a high pedestal, so close inspection was impossible. (It does seems quite stupid that cities so often put statues of great men beyond the range of ordinary eyesight - Nelson's Column is an extreme example.) But since this statue was only made in 1872, and the historical Leonardo is something of a mythical figure, the sculptor is unlikely to have created a perfect likeness. I waited for several minutes, even so, hoping to take a photograph *without* a pigeon sitting on the statue's head, but had to give up.

Despite having been led to expect that the La Scala opera house would be less than grand in external appearance, we still felt for a moment that we must have the wrong building. I had first heard of it way back in the very early fifties, when Mario Lanza was bringing opera to the masses through his films and recordings, much as the three tenors have been doing in more recent years. Given the austere times, I would say he was more successful, too. I certainly got the opera bug for awhile, even though I was only in my early teens. Indeed, one of the most exciting moments of my young life was sitting down in the best cinema in town to watch the film of *The Great Caruso*. It certainly seems odd now, but what little knowledge I have of opera - confined to being able to recognise the more famous arias for tenor - dates from that time. When *Nessun Dorma* became the anthem for the football World Cup I already knew it by heart, even though I hadn't listened to it for nearly forty years. As a relief from the prevailing social circumstances, films in those days sought to convey a world of glamorous opulence rather than gritty realism, so part of my mind (I am assuming that Mario Lanza was filmed on the actual La Scala stage) had still expected it to be a place of sumptuous extravagance, both inside and out. In fact indoors it did resemble more closely my old vision. There were no rehearsals going on, so we were able to wander about and sit in the plush boxes more or less at will. For those with a deeper interest in opera than mine nowadays, there is an excellent museum containing objects and relics relating to La Scala's history, and in particular a fine collection of Verdi memorabilia. There is also a small shop where we bought postcards to send to opera-loving friends in the States.

To reach the Piazza del Duomo you pass conveniently through the Galleria Vittorio Emanuele, and so can indulge in a little harmless window shopping as a relief from (somewhat) higher things. In fact we did have one shopping requirement. My wife has a favourite perfume: *Missoni*. The special merits of this or any other label are rather lost in me, given my extreme lack of sensitivity in the nasal department; but she is enthusiastic about *Missoni* almost to the exclusion of all other fragrances. At Christmas and birthday times, though, it was becoming quite impossible to track down in England. Her supply in fact was running dangerously low - hence the switch now to the country of origin. We couldn't find any in the grand arcade, however, and had to continue the search later.

I had stood in front of too many magnificent cathedrals to say that Milan's took my breath away, but it is a stupendous creation, more intricately decorated than any other I have seen. Its forest of slender spires are the most distinctive feature - you think at once of Oxford and the talk of "dreaming spires". In fact because of the massiveness of the building, they might be better described as bristling. Inside I had the same sense of the sheer *quality* of everything experienced years before in St Peter's. For those with macabre tastes there is a particularly interesting statue of St Bartholomew, after flaying. In the great and stoical tradition of saints, at least as depicted in religious works of art, the man is up and about his business with little concern for his extra dimension of nakedness. Otherwise enjoying the cathedral was as always chiefly a matter of staring upwards in wonder.

Outside in the square there were the usual vast numbers of pigeons. In a country so hungry apparently for bird flesh, they lead an extraordinarily charmed life. Are they inedible?

We came upon a shop or business premises a little later actually bearing the name "Missoni". Since, however, it's a brand name or designer label for a range of products amongst which their perfume is of perhaps minor importance, they couldn't actually sell us any. But they knew a lady who could. And so that particular search turned out not to be in vain.

By now we were well into the afternoon and it was time to pay our respects to Leonardo's famous painting of The Last Supper. We had checked the guidebooks with some care to ascertain when exactly this masterpiece could be viewed. Because of its extremely poor and deteriorating condition, access was understandably limited. Directions as to where precisely it was housed were less clear in the guides; we knew only that it had to be somewhere in the immediate vicinity of the church of Santa Maria delle Grazie. This I laboriously located on our street plan - though in truth it was only a matter of sticking to the main road (the Corso Megenta), heading west from the cathedral. We expected the painting to be somewhere in the church itself. Only after we had hunted around and drawn a puzzling blank did we scrutinise the guidebooks more closely. The elementary fact was that The Last Supper was a *fresco*, and therefore could not be carted off somewhere else or put into storage. It had to be permanently on a wall in one of the buildings associated with the church.

I had definitely read that the painting was in a convent, but our best guide now indicated that it occupied the end wall of the refectory of a former Dominican *monastery*. Which was true? Were they simply different historical usages for the same building? And why in any case were there no signs anywhere to point us in the right direction, or explanatory notices on doors or outbuildings? Why, too, did we appear to be the only people in Milan interested in seeing The Last Supper on this particular afternoon?

We poked about again in and around the church, but the only possible clue was a part of a room that had been screened off with heavy, near-impenetrable canvas material. Whatever was behind was in darkness, so even where we could find a chink in the protective curtain, we could only guess at what was concealed. That might be a hopeful sign, though. It would make sense if the fresco was being protected from the harmful effect of exposure to light during the hours when it wasn't on public view. Why at this moment it *was* out of sight we couldn't yet understand, since we had come at a time when access ought to have been permissible; but then perhaps viewing was by request only. Leonardo was known to have experimented with radical methods to avoid having to use the established fresco technique of painting directly onto wet plaster, which didn't allow him to work at his preferred slow pace. The result was that the paint had begun to flake off almost before he had put down his brushes. Nearly five hundred years later, it was a miracle that anything was left of the original work at all. Obviously the priceless remnants had to be treated with the utmost care.

Well, finally we found someone to ask and were told matter-of-factly that there was no viewing today. We complained loudly that our guidebook said differently, and that we had come all the way from England to see the painting; but set against the health of a precious fifteenth-century Renaissance masterpiece our protests amounted to scarcely audible squeaks. We never did find out if The Last Supper really was behind the crude protective curtain. I suspect not.

After that disappointment we hadn't the heart or energy to explore the city further and made our way back to the station, arriving too soon for our train. The timetable showed that we could if we wished take an earlier Inter City. There was a supplementary charge, but as seasoned travellers we were quite confident that we would be able to pay this on the train itself. In the event, however, the ticket collector demanded on-the-spot payment of a hefty fine - we ought to have paid the extra charge in Milan. What made this particular wrangle especially annoying was that there were some French students in our compartment (at least they *said* that's what they were, though they looked older) who had made the same mistake. To our amazement and great indignation they were simply allowed to get away with it, while the man indicated that if *we* didn't pay up the consequences would be very serious indeed. The day had not been an unqualified success, though we had the perfume and some memories of a fine city. And there was the short ferry trip still to come. In the end we shrugged our shoulders over the fine. If you can't do that in Italy you don't belong there. (And besides, it didn't sound nearly so hefty in English money!)

On our last day, despite threatening black clouds and a strong wind blowing up, we couldn't resist a last visit for lunch to Pescatori. This time we had to eat indoors as a fierce storm soon developed, buffeting the tiny island so that you felt it might actually capsize and sink to the bottom of the lake. We had the restaurant, indeed the island, to ourselves. The avenue of trees shook and shutters rattled, but we rode out the tempest in the most pleasant of circumstances, enjoying the kind of meal you can only dream about back home.

CHAPTER 10

SORRENTO - 1994

When you have been once to Sorrento, even if it is not precisely your favourite place in the world, you are always aware of an inner commitment to return one day. You remember that last glimpse from the coach window, and of course the famous song is always playing somewhere in the recesses of your mind. One day you feel sure you will go back, though you don't necessarily make firm plans. It can seem to happen accidentally. Late in 1994, an expensive tour of Virginia and Chesapeake Bay taken in the spring with Washington friends having begun to fade, we were finding the pull of Italy difficult to resist once more. But funds were low. Sorrento proved to be almost the only destination available. The travel agent found an excellent deal for us, however, and in what sounded like a first-rate hotel, the Sorrento Palace. And so a few days later there we were again, just as we had always known we would be one day. Routine stuff, of course; but modern travel can still seem like a small miracle if like me you only began to go abroad with any frequency in early middle age.

Much had happened back in England since our 1986 visit. The money-craziness of the late eighties had turned the most ordinary of mortals into wide-eyed share-owning democrats, and almost everyone had believed for awhile that house prices could rise steeply more or less indefinitely. We had even tried to scramble aboard the mad runaway express ourselves, but by good luck our deal fell through. Then had come the so-easily predictable collapse of confidence, and the painful anxieties of the recession years. Institutions and social goals taken for granted by those who had grown up with the Welfare State, already seriously undermined during the boom, were now under further and possibly terminal attack. I hated what was happening, but I have to say that we as a family had done pretty well out of the roller-coaster years. By 1994 Rebecca was finding her feet as a teacher, Suzanne was at university, my wife was now working part time but was still earning good money in her job, and while I was facing imminent redundancy myself, there would be generous compensation, and I would be half-glad in any case to escape from a new business culture that was increasingly alien to me.

And no doubt the Italians had been through their own traumas. Indeed, for them there seems to be no respite from political crises and turmoil, even when times are supposed to be good. But I have to confess that we don't make a study of their problems. Perhaps away from the tourist centres shops were boarded up and people were sleeping rough, much as in certain English towns and cities; but Sorrento looked much the same as when we had left it. And there was nothing for it but to accept what we saw. That's one of the truly pleasurable things about visiting a favourite foreign country whose language you don't speak very well: unless you're a masochist you don't have to get emotionally caught up in matters that you can't possibly influence anyhow. There's enough of that sort of wearing futility back home. You can't help noticing, too, that despite the endless political turmoil things seem able to go on pretty much as normal - in places like Sorrento, at any rate.

The Sorrento Palace is situated high above the old town. It has a wavy balcony frontage, below which is an elaborately conceived swimming pool - sadly too cold for us in November. There is also a peaceful orchard which offers escape from the crowds, should there be any. In point of fact we found the guest population of the hotel remarkably variable. Some days the vast lobby could be deserted, but then great armies of Americans or Japanese would suddenly arrive, usually on a very tight schedule. They would be milling around reception and would show up later at dinner, but by next morning they would have disappeared without trace. The Americans in particular, often elderly, were quite extraordinary in their energy and their ability to rise before dawn in good time for the day's events. If you chanced to study the notice boards you could be staggered by what was arranged for them. Besides breakfast and the other routine morning requirements, they might have an Italian lesson to take in, followed by a keep-fit session, and perhaps a dip in the indoor pool - then be packed and ready to board their coach to move on to Milan or somewhere by, say, six-thirty - long before we had so much as opened an eye. These phenomenal Americans made not the smallest concession to age. If you looked at some of them closely you felt they must be approaching a hundred, yet they would be togged out in bright summer beach wear, as if this was Hawaii. The Japanese by contrast were apt to be suited and slothful. Inside the hotel there was nothing to point their cameras at, so they could seem a bit lost.

The travel writer Bill Bryson, when he was passing through the area a few years ago gathering material for his book of European travels *Neither Here Nor There*, stopped at the hotel Eden, which I don't remember seeing. He tells us that he fell instantly in love with Sorrento. This was perhaps as well because he seems to have spent hardly a day in the town. His thumbnail description, composed one cannot tell when, is that it "tumbles down from the station to the Bay of Naples". In point of fact if you were to attempt to walk from the station to the sea - and it's a walk of about half a kilometre - you would eventually tumble off the towering cliffs, which are Sorrento's most arresting natural feature. He picks out the Piazza Tasso for special mention and praise. Maybe the old sign guiding visitors to the "Rovers Return Inn" (highly visible when we were first there in 1986) had been removed by the time he called by. But in general I love Bryson's books, and if I am introducing a sour note here it is partly because of their great success, but also because of his remarks about middle-aged English tourists having an off-season holiday - that is one they could afford. He writes that everywhere he went in Sorrento (and in the time available he could not have roamed very far) he kept seeing these English couples, the wife looking critically at everything and the man dragging along behind. Usually they would be involved in some petty squabble. Well, of course none of this could possibly apply to *us*. But Bryson gives every impression in his books of being a happy family man himself. His own children must now be growing and soon he and his wife will also be free to visit these holiday places as a middle-aged couple. I look forward to bumping into the Brysons on their travels a few years from now, especially if I should happen to be gathering material for a new book of my own.

We did not in any case envisage spending much time in the town on this visit. Instead we planned to do some serious walking, and the high position of the Sorrento Palace gave us a good start, bearing in mind that escape from Sorrento on foot is bound to be uphill whichever way you go. We had thoughts of crossing the peninsula, which looks quite narrow on the map - only about four kilometres coast to coast. That should be no more than a morning's stroll, even allowing for the rugged terrain. We had also read about a network of Roman roads or footpaths that were being opened up for walkers, and hoped they might prove useful.

On our first outing we set ourselves the modest objective of reaching the hill town of St Agata, situated at roughly the midpoint. The early stages were fairly easy, if steeply uphill; we stuck to the modern roads where we could. But the makers of these roads have ignored the Roman example, for they twist and turn all over the place so as to avoid the steepest gradients. If you follow them you begin to doubt if they are taking you in the right direction, and at times they may even go downhill for a bit. Losing altitude is the last thing you want to do. So then you begin to look for reasonably well-worn paths that will at least keep you moving upwards. But as on any walk, paths can lead nowhere. The hillside vegetation in Italy is not luxuriant, but it can be dense and at times impenetrable. Thus you can become ever more trapped or lost - and hot and scratched, too - until you are forced to think about retracing your steps, which is itself never easy. Either that or you hit another road going in what seems the wrong direction again, or with a gradient contrary to what you would have expected. Then all you have left for guidance is the sun. All that describes in general terms our experience for the first couple of hours of this ramble, but eventually we reached a point where we believed we must surely be close at last to St Agata. And just at that moment we saw for the first time other people, much younger than ourselves, coming downhill in the opposite direction.

In a foreign country it can sometimes be hard to recognise your compatriots. (This happens most often in hotel lifts, especially in one-to-one situations.) So we made way for these younger folk to pass with a few tentative words of Italian - until at last one of them spoke and we discovered they were from Preston. We discussed home matters for awhile before enquiring where precisely they were heading (*back* from somewhere, we presumed). "St Agata," they told us. They were of course as lost as we were, even though they had a copy of the map of the old Roman footpaths from the tourist office. We were able, however, to combine intelligence, and after a few more confusing moments found our way to our shared objective. My wife and I sat wearily on a bench in front of the church for a bit, while our new and more energetic friends had a look around. Then we found a nice little *trattoria* for lunch.

While we two felt well satisfied with the morning's exertions, to the point where we considered the day virtually over from a walking point of view (going back, if we had to walk, would be downhill all the way), it emerged that the younger people - a brother and sister, we gathered, plus girlfriend (whose we weren't sure) - were ambitious to complete the crossing of the peninsula before darkness fell. They had checked that the local bus service - which passed through

St Agata itself - picked up other villages they knew of, vaguely to the south and west. With that information, plus the map of the old Roman footpaths to guide them in the descent ahead, they saw no great difficulty. After a glass or two of wine we decided to join them, persuaded in part by the argument that there was safety in numbers.

So, pressing on, we took a minor road down towards the village of Torca. From there the young man was sure that a coastal path existed which would take us westward towards the tip of the peninsula, besides offering cliff-top views comparable to the Amalfi Drive. The other villages on the bus route - Nerano was one - were in that general direction, he said. But even reaching Torca proved less than straightforward, and after that we got hopelessly lost in a maze of paths with stone walls and fences, which were attractive in themselves but seemed designed more to provide access to allotments than for pedestrian through-traffic. We knew by now that somewhere up above us to the north was the bus-service road, but no path seemed to take us towards it. At length we began to make rather desperate enquiries. Here, though, we were only talking to gardeners, who could make no sense at all of what we were saying. *"Dov'è la strada?"* was a funny question to ask, I suppose, in the middle of a patchwork of allotments. Our last resort once more was that old aid to navigation, the sun - even if it would only be with us for another couple of hours at most. Trespassing on private property and climbing over obstacles as they confronted us, we headed north without deviation. That way we knew we couldn't in the end fail to find the road, provided we were determined enough.

It took about another half hour, even so. My wife and I felt we had been through some kind of survival course and only wanted to climb the kilometre or so back to St Agata to catch a bus or take a taxi to Sorrento as necessary; but the younger people were still keen to press on with the original plan. We left them to it, much as adventurers part company with their more suicidal companions on polar expeditions, hardly expecting to see them again. But when our bus, which had been a long time coming, paused for no more than a moment somewhere near Nerano, they scrambled aboard, grinning with pleasure. By then it was almost dark.

A few days later we visited Nerano ourselves - by bus. Part of the attraction was that we believed we would have a good view from there of Capri, which is only a very short distance off the tip of the peninsula. Unfortunately there was a small mountain smack in between. We weren't in the mood for climbing, and thought of trying to skirt around the obstacle. To the south were impassable cliffs, so that way was out of the question. In the other direction there was a winding path up to the village of San Constanzo and beyond. It looked promising enough to be worth following for awhile; but the climb was increasingly steep, and each time we glanced back the bulk of the mountain seemed to be just as massively in the way. So we gave up and instead began to look for somewhere nice for lunch. Way down back at beach level we found a near-empty eating establishment with a rustic verandah and rather more plush interior, offering chiefly fish. The place was overrun with cats, and you immediately suspected a connection. The speciality of the house was a fresh-fish dish, which we decided to try, hoping for a substantial fish steak. In the event we each got a plateful of small fried sea creatures of many kinds, all of them whole, complete with eyes and all other vital organs, and entirely recognisable for what they were. I'm sure the dish was actually of the highest quality, but it did bear some resemblance to the floor sweepings of an aquarium. Fortunately we had ordered a plate of chips, plus salad and bread (and wine and mineral water), so we were able to drop much of the main dish to the cats around our feet when no one was looking without having to leave the table hungry. They all looked very healthy and contented. Half way back to Sorrento, our companions of the earlier trek once again clambered aboard the bus.

Next morning, rather than try to find another mainland spot from which to look across at Capri, we decided to do the obvious (something we hadn't managed in 1986) and take the short ferry ride to the island. After only a minute or two we rounded the headland and there it was - sheer rocky outcrops rising out of green lower slopes, with white dwellings dotted above a small harbour town. Like many other visitors (Bill Bryson included), we imagined we had only to step off the boat to be in the heart of the place. In fact Capri town is a few kilometres away up in the hills. Fortunately for us (Bryson had to reach it on foot) the *funicolare* was operating, though there was an uninviting queue. Also touting for business were assorted taxis and other drivers, offering anything from short lifts to full tours of the island - at a price. One of the ferry passengers was already bargaining with a driver and trying to round up others to make the trip economical. We began to show some interest, but then the *funicolare* suddenly removed most of the queuing people so he ducked out, leaving the rest of us to placate the poor driver (he had all four doors of his car open and waiting) with polite bows, spreading of open palms and shrugging of shoulders - and perhaps even a small tip.

In the centre of Capri town was the cosy little Piazza Umberto Primo, with its shops and cafés and the backdrop of the church of Santo Stefano. It's a place for milling around - always the favourite activity of tourists, at a pace dictated by the slowest in the throng. After milling in the square for a bit, we moved up the steps alongside the church to mill more extensively. There were more shops, chiefly of the up-market designer-label kind. But we also stumbled upon a little *profumeria*, which my wife entered for only a moment and then emerged from triumphantly flourishing her favourite *Missoni* brand. In spite of this little bit of good fortune (for she was again running out of the precious fragrance), I confess that I was not as enthralled as I would have expected to be by Capri town, or by what I had seen so far of the rest of the island. It was attractive enough, but to me not very *Italian*. Instead, I was put in mind (though I've never visited one) of a *Greek* island. But we of course made the most of it, exploring the little lanes and passageways - everywhere white and bright and adorned with the ubiquitous bougainvillea - climbed stone steps to try to find a little solitude or a better scenic viewing point, and otherwise mooched and milled and mingled until we had had our fill and decided to move on by bus to Anacapri.

I had been looking forward, rather secretly, to this part of the visit, because I simply could not understand how Anacapri could be reached by land. The rocky inland cliffs, seen from the ferry as you approached the harbour, had appeared to span the entire width of the island, and yet the maps clearly showed that Anacapri was beyond them.

The escarpment looked intriguingly like the edge of a lost or forbidden world, beyond which dinosaurs, or King Kong himself, might dwell. But I could tell as the bus set off that I was alone in having such thoughts; not even my wife seemed much interested in the mystery. This rather spoiled things, because I knew there would have to be a mundane explanation. So I tried to suppress ideas such as that the driver himself (who would obviously be making the journey several times a day) might actually stop his bus at the foot of the cliff and confess himself baffled, or that he might shout a magical command and cause a great door to open and allow us through. Instead I idly waited to see what would in fact happen, and of course the road meandered over to one extreme end of the escarpment (the right-hand end from our position) and somehow sneaked around the edge, giving us another of those giddying window views that had me reaching for the camera.

Anacapri was much quieter - rather deserted, in fact. We were by now well into the afternoon and hadn't yet had lunch, so we did little more than find a pleasant balcony restaurant overlooking a peaceful square. To our surprise, in spite of there being almost no one about, a man in ordinary workman's clothes just across from us began to play a guitar - seemingly for his own enjoyment, or perhaps he was rehearsing for the next rush of tourists. Anyway, no sooner had he begun than another man, who seemed to have no connection with the first, strolled over from another part of the square and began to sing along. It was a folk song of some kind, though not one we knew. Then others - singers and musicians - joined in. The performance seemed entirely spontaneous, so that you felt the people of Anacapri must be so contented with life that they couldn't resist making music when the slightest excuse occurred. I need hardly say that a part of my mind expected an indication after a couple of songs that a small payment for the entertainment would be very welcome, but it didn't happen. Before we had even finished our meal the musicians casually disbanded and went about their business without so much as a word to one another.

Back on the mainland, the extensive and leisurely walking we had planned rather eluded us. As with the trek to St Agata and beyond, our rambles tended to run into difficulties. One morning we set out for the Capo di Sorrento, which juts out into the Bay of Naples at the western end of the town. There were supposed to be clear footpaths down from the high road, but we could find no trace of them. Instead, to escape from the traffic, we were obliged to turn inland and were soon lost in a maze of paths and minor roads, eventually finding ourselves with a fine view

- perhaps the best we had ever enjoyed - of Sorrento; but no way back that we could see. At this point we got into conversation with another English couple who confirmed that the descent from our present position would not be easy. They knew this because their hotel, to which they were at that moment returning after a morning ramble, was way up there in the hills and they had to use a bus service to reach town. But the daft thing was that because they were such pleasant company, we casually walked with then almost as far as their hotel, all of us knowing it would be a dead end as far as we were concerned. We may have had in mind taking a bus ourselves, I don't remember. If so, it didn't happen. We had lunch that day at about four o'clock.

Another long walk did prove a little easier in the physical sense, being all on one level, and more straightforward from the navigational point of view, too, since we stuck strictly to roads and had a good map. We simply walked the full length of what I think of as the Sorrento plateau; though the town itself occupies only a part of it, the rest no doubt being classified technically as suburbs. The walk took us first into St Agnello, where we made a large detour to have a fresh look at the streets around the Hotel Mediterraneo, in which we had stayed with our friends eight years before, when the children were all children. As might be expected, since we were way out of season, the area was very quiet, with few of the little cafés that had specialised in bacon, egg and chips open for business, and the hotel itself actually closed. From there, with a hint of rain in the air, we continued through less clearly defined districts as far as Meta and the start of the long main-road climb from which coach travellers take their last fond backward glance. None of it, alas, was very memorable, with the exception of a tiny fishing village we paused in on the return walk. But paused is the wrong word, since we had to descend a series of steep contrary slopes to reach the bottom of the cliffs. The village consisted of little more than a single short street and a small marina. It was all rather shabby and untidy, but we took that as a positive sign that we had discovered somewhere as yet untouched by tourism. Now all we needed was an authentic fish restaurant, the prospect of which had indeed been our chief motivation for making the descent. But the sad thing is that the little places you happen to find which tourism has not yet touched or has passed by, especially one as small as this, simply don't set up the sort of restaurant we were hoping for just to feed themselves. It's the despised tourists who make such places possible. So we had to climb all the way back to the cliff tops unfed; and now, having threatened us all morning, the rain began to fall - great big drops, only a single one of which could leave you soaking. We did our best to shelter between showers till we at last reached St Agnello station and a train to take us back into town.

It was an active couple of weeks, when I look back. We managed a repeat rail trip to Pompeii, which was far easier to cope with in the cooler weather, and much less busy, though the condition of the roads hadn't improved. In a remote part of the site we noticed an elderly man - American by the look of it - who was alone but clearly having a very special experience. It would be no exaggeration to say that his face was aglow with pleasure. He was looking very intently at even the most obscure ruined dwellings and exploring their interiors with great reverence.

His behaviour was made more poignant by the fact that he was short of breath and struggling to negotiate awkward entrances, broken steps and the like. He also bore a quite striking resemblance to the American writer Kurt Vonnegut, whose books I happened to be deeply into just then; though this did not seem the right territory for a writer whose novels tend towards science fiction. But we felt concerned enough - and I had sufficient curiosity - to engage him in conversation. Well, it wasn't Kurt Vonnegut, of course, but a professor from an American university - out west somewhere, I think. We stayed with him awhile and did our best to show interest in what he had to say about the things immediately confronting us, though we could tell that we were probably spoiling his afternoon. He had been to Pompeii several times previously, but this visit was a very special one, he told us, without quite explaining why. We couldn't help as a result feeling more concerned for his health than ever - was he thinking of *dying* there? - but didn't want to get in his way any longer and so left him to stagger on along the broken streets alone. Later in the day we were much relieved to bump into him again on the Corso Italia, back in Sorrento.

We had three small bites at Naples, a city you would not of course want to risk getting lost in. Our first visit was on an organised excursion from our hotel. The weather was wet and cool, and the place looked shabby and gloomy; though this could have been because our driver had a preference for backstreet routes. It may have been a Sunday. There weren't many people about, at any rate, not even in their cars. The main event was a visit to the National Archaeological Museum, a collection of world importance; but it's amazing how time (in this case only a couple of years) can wipe such experiences from the memory. I expect we were simply exposed to a surfeit of archaeological treasures. None of it registered, but I haven't forgotten sprinting back to the coach through a torrential and perhaps even life-threatening downpour.

Nor have I forgotten our visit afterwards to the Solfatara - the dusty yellowish crater of a half-extinct (does that make it safe?) volcano near Pozzuoli, only a few kilometres from the city. Notwithstanding its supposedly slumbering condition, the crater was emitting sulphurous smoke and hot bubbling mud of a worrying reddish-purple colour. Fortunately the rain had stopped, or it might well have added to the chemical fermentation. I was reminded of those space-probe pictures we see of the topography of Venus. Parts of the site were fenced off, but we were able to wander with surprising freedom, the main restriction being the temperature in places of the surface underfoot (I hesitate to use the word ground).

What made the visit truly memorable, though, was something trivial again. We were accompanied everywhere by a multi-coloured, and in the circumstances remarkably clean and healthy-looking, cat. The creature wasn't much interested in making friends; it simply liked to follow people around the strange and inhospitable landscape at a safe distance - perhaps in the hope one day of seeing the crater open up and swallow a visitor or two, who can tell? Its feet must have been made of asbestos.

Our other two brief visits to Naples - both on the same day - were unintentional. We set out to take the ferry to the island of Ischia. It went via Naples, where we mistakenly believed (or were told by someone) that we would have to change to a different boat. Of course we realised too late that we should have stayed aboard. But we now had a little time to size up the truly massive Castel Nuovo, which was right there down near the waterfront. This dark, forbidding fortress is nowadays used as little more than an administrative block, we were disappointed to learn. We were also able to stroll around the harbour square before the next ferry was due, but didn't notice much of special interest.

Ischia reminded us of Elba, back in 1980. Hardly anything or anyone was open for business. Paying for bus rides in Italy can be difficult. You have to do it in advance, buying tickets from a tobacconist or other authorised shop. But no such establishment was available. So we got on a bus anyway, going we knew not where, but determined to brazen it out if confronted. At first there was some safety in numbers, but to our dismay the passengers began to get off at each succeeding stop, with no new ones replacing them (a mystery in itself - was the driver returning to the depot, and if so where was it?). Soon we were the only ones left, at which point we rather lost our nerve and leapt off ourselves, in the middle of nowhere. Now we were really stranded. What we needed more than anything was a nice *trattoria*, from which, after dining, we could have called for a taxi to return us to the harbour; but there was nothing remotely of that sort to be seen. Then another bus came along, travelling the opposite way; so we boarded that, convinced that our little adventure on Ischia was already over. To our surprise, however, the new bus veered off in a totally new direction, and proceeded to take us for a scenic tour of the whole island, lasting about an hour. We were the only passengers, and after a time the driver appeared even to lose interest in making stops. Whether or not we had tickets seemed to be of no concern whatever to him.

Back at the quayside, we expected to be able to take a ferry direct to Sorrento; but the only one available now (and it was only late afternoon) was back to Naples - and not to the harbour we had left but to Mergillina, which is further north. Arriving with dusk beginning to fall, we lost no time in summoning a taxi to take us to the main station, little realising that we were about to have one of those driving experiences you never ever forget.

There was a broad avenue along the sea front - three lanes each way, separated by tramlines - with the traffic seemingly close to gridlock. We were hungry and began to think in terms of late trains and the near certainty of missing dinner back at the Sorrento Palace; but our young driver simply didn't acknowledge the congestion. Instead, with a single hand on the wheel and his foot hard down, he drove unflinchingly into it, veering expertly back and forth across all three lanes - plus occasionally the tramlines themselves - to exploit the smallest and most fleeting gaps. What we saw from our rear seat was like the back projection for a Keystone Cops movie. Vehicles would rise up for brief moments right smack in front of us, only to reappear again behind when we dared to open our eyes. But the whole performance was incredibly cool rather than recklessly mad. The driver was chatting to base on his radio for most of the time. At length we reached a junction where we could see he would have to cross the equally dense opposing streams of traffic. There were lights, though in Naples that meant nothing. We braced ourselves for certain death - but without ever exposing us to real danger he proceeded to inch his way across the fast flowing lanes, forcing them one by one to halt and let him across. Reaching the station defeated him, however, strange to say. There was simply no way through the last bit. We were wondering if he might actually try to drive over the car rooftops, when he suddenly swung off the road onto a rough patch of ground - full of apologies and pointing out that the station was now in sight. Hand shaking, I gave him a generous tip.

CHAPTER 11

TAORMINA - 1996

Books about the Italian peninsula and its islands should probably *begin* with Sicily. Goethe wrote some considerable time ago that it was impossible to understand Italy without knowing this island. Its turbulent history, together with the never-ending exposure to natural disasters, more than match anything the mainland (or Continental Italy, as the natives are said to refer to it) can offer, for those who like to contemplate centuries of pain, hardship and general suffering. And all this testing experience has produced a special breed of men, they say: at times proud and aloof, dark and brooding; more often warm and generous - a fascinating amalgam of all the many characteristics of the races who have by turns ruled the island and been driven from its shores. Indeed, from the literature, there seems to be no aspect of the human personality that has not been incorporated into the Sicilian character. To be thus burdened must be a difficult thing. So it is hardly surprising, on the face of it, if your waiter seems less than gracious when you order a *cappuccino* at a table on the Corso Umberto in Taormina. But I confess that I am not a great believer in this idea of the immutable national character or soul. The feeling in our party at the end of this holiday was that the Sicilians were different from other Italians; less friendly, certainly. But everyone also agreed that they were not yet fully geared to tourism. Adapting to these latest and softest invaders, armed with nothing more menacing than their fat wallets and happy credit cards, may be taking a little time. Perhaps the Sicilians can't quite believe their good luck, after so many centuries of contending with murderous sea pirates of one kind or another - not to mention the murderous Mount Etna (known locally as Mongibello) forever blowing off. But I feel sure that with patience they will learn to suppress the inward protests of their complex, troublesome souls and become just as deft and cheerful as those who take money from tourists everywhere. I know from experience that the *Yugoslavs* were beginning to get the hang of it, just before their country fell apart.

In our twenty years of foreign travel we have been very lucky with flight arrangements. On a couple of occasions we have had delays with return flights (once, supposedly returning from Pisa, we had to take a coach transfer through the night to Bologna); but for the most part we have had no great difficulty putting up with the occasional bit of inconvenience. Sometimes an extra few hours abroad can seem distinctly preferable to a punctual return to a grey and drizzly Manchester. So I have always listened with impatience to people's tales of flight delays, feeling that they should appreciate what a privilege it is for them, as very ordinary mortals who by the purest chance happen to be living in a very fortunate age, to have the opportunity to get on an aeroplane at all. The fact is that neither of my parents ever came close to it, and I can't recall my grandparents so much as enjoying a ride on a *train*.

But I have done too much flying not to have to confess that even for me there are limits. From an early stage we had doubts as to whether this trip to Sicily would actually happen. Flights to Italy (other than the scheduled kind) can be erratic at the best of times, especially out of Manchester; and we were going right at the end of the season. The name of the airline was new to us, too. Several times we received advice through the post of changed flight details, and then only the day before departure we were told that our return flight would now be via Gatwick, with seemingly precious little time to make the necessary transfer. We were quite unprepared for difficulties with the outward flight, however. We might not have minded so much if we hadn't had to rise from our bed at four in the morning.

At first all we knew of the difficulties was the plain stated fact of a three-hour delay on the departure screens. On seeing that we decided to stroll across to one of the nearby hotels for a leisurely breakfast. But the service was very efficient and we soon found ourselves back in the departure lounge - just in time to hear an announcement that a free cooked breakfast was now being served for passengers on our delayed flight. Fortunately WH Smith's was by now open, so we bought newspapers and magazines and made ourselves as comfortable as we could in crowded circumstances. Next, not long before our revised flight time, came the announcement of a further substantial delay; and at the same time rumours began to circulate that we were to be taken to a hotel for lunch. By now everyone (we were beginning to know one another) felt entitled to an explanation. At the desk dealing with airport information we were told that the plane which should by this time have landed us in Catania had, it was thought, been diverted to Luton on a return flight from Greece, because of a riot on board. An alternative reason offered for the delay was that one of the company's aircraft had been grounded for technical reasons, so that they were trying to meet all their commitments with one plane short. The lady at the desk was so sorry, but we would soon be bussed across to a good hotel for lunch. Our departure was by now expected to be in the late afternoon.

It all sounds terrible - and no doubt terribly familiar - but I believe that for most people in this kind of situation there are unacknowledged compensations. The fact is that the worse things get for the passenger (or customer), the more *important* he becomes. A delay of only a few hours means that he personally can demand a convincing explanation, at the very least. And if the situation gets a lot worse than that he can begin to draft in his mind the strong letter of complaint that he will most assuredly fire off the moment he returns from this wretched holiday. In his wildest fantasies, he might even have the pleasure of imagining a direct confrontation with the accursed company's chief executive. And another bonus is that such experiences do bring people together. Whereas you would normally go through the procedures of boarding an aircraft with little more than a glance at your fellow passengers; after a few hours of being mucked about as we were on that Saturday morning you are practically on first-name terms. What's more, we had the extra benefit of a really rotten lunch. I won't name the hotel, but we certainly expected better from them. It added enormously to our feelings of comradeship. My wife and I had experienced nothing like it since our trip to Russia in the late eighties.

We were surprised to discover, given the near-limitless opportunity for conversation, that many of our comrades in adversity were like ourselves on their umpteenth visit to Italy. Without having a burning interest in its art, history, culture, or any special aspect of Italian life, they too had experienced a growing love for and identification with the country, to the point where they seldom went anywhere else on holiday. We felt we were among friends. Most of us had been planning a visit to Sicily for some years, but for various reasons - the Mafia; the expense; the heat - had been putting it off. In our group, too, were several people with relatives out there. The most memorable of these was a voluble American of Sicilian ancestry who lived in Ireland but had relatives in Manchester. He was flying out at short notice in response to a vacation offer from the Sicilian branch of his extended family. With the help of a few drinks the companionship became increasingly enjoyable, so that it was almost a shame when we at last got the call to board our plane. It took off nearly ten hours late.

This, I need hardly explain, was another package tour. Quite when we began to turn away from self-organised holidays in Italy, and to settle instead for the convenience of having things mostly arranged in advance, I'm not sure. I dislike the idea of being labelled as just an ordinary holiday-maker or tourist. It is difficult, however, to think of yourself as a serious traveller when you have pre-booked two full weeks half-board in a good three-star hotel. We had a strong desire to explore the island as much as we could alone, but also a feeling that we were doubtless being unrealistic. If you are nervous about getting lost in the suburbs of Naples, how very much more terrifying it would be to lose your bearings in Palermo, or to wander accidentally off the civilised track somewhere in Sicily's dark and menacing interior, close perhaps to the infamous town of Corleone. But the truth was that we didn't even plan to hire a car, and Taormina is a long way from both Palermo and Corleone. Any private exploring we might wish to undertake would have to be by train or bus.

Our first view of the town was late at night, by which time we were dog-tired. So not much registered, except perhaps for the roads, which seemed extraordinarily tortuous even by Italian standards as they climbed steeply up from the coast. Next morning we stepped out onto our balcony, which amounted almost to a small garden, and found that we had a marvellous view along a craggy receding coastline, north towards Messina. Perched on a hilltop a few kilometres away was the picturesque town of Forza d'Agro, while across the water the mainland - specifically the extremity of the toe of Italy in the region of Calabria - was clearly visible. The view was spoiled just a little by the even more visible *autostrada*, snaking along the shoreline; the much closer supports and cables of the *funivia*, which carried people endlessly down to and up from the beach area; and the brown and barren appearance of much of the immediate landscape. But that is not to say that we did not feel extremely fortunate.

It was only on leaving our hotel (the Sirius) next morning, however, that we began to appreciate what a breathtaking place Taormina is. We went along, with some reluctance, to the starting point for an introductory guided town tour - although I do notice in myself now a worrying readiness to submit to appetisers of this kind. Maybe they are actually useful.

Our first stop was the celebrated Greek Theatre. This was an amazing place - not so much the amphitheatre and other substantial ruins (chiefly Roman) as the whole setting. We had there our first clear view of Mount Etna, only about thirty kilometres away to the summit. The layout of the arena seemed designed with the volcano in mind as a central backdrop, but the curious thing was that the alignment wasn't quite right. Maybe the mountain had shifted. Our guide said that the Greeks were supposed to have had no awareness of the beauty or significance of landscape and so the position of Etna as a perfect stage backdrop may have been accidental. But they certainly had their myths about the volcano, imagining it as the forge of Vulcan, God of fire, and the home of the Cyclopes, the one-eyed cannibal giants encountered by Odysseus. So it would hardly be surprising if these myths were incorporated into the stories being enacted on stage. Indeed, one can easily imagine the real volcano, perhaps with primitive but dramatic stage effects, having a starring role. The Romans too were very conscious of Etna's presence, though they would seem to have been chiefly concerned about its power to distract audiences from the spectacular and gory events being served up, no doubt at great expense, for their special delectation in the arena. In fact in converting the place for their own purposes, they made extensive alterations, now extensively demolished, which obscured the volcano from view.

From these rosy ruins, and more particularly from the terraces of the great amphitheatre, besides the commanding view of Etna there were other magnificent sights all around and up and down. In fact you hardly knew which way to point your eyes. To the rear, rising abruptly from the sometimes green and wooded lower slopes, were dramatic rocky outcrops - one topped by the ruins of an old castle; another, glimpsed beyond, the scarcely believable site of the perilously perched small town of Castelmola, which looked unreachable on foot. And spreading out into the middle distance was much of the high town of Taormina; while far below were the cliffs, coastal towns and the blue sea, receding southwards towards Catania.

But so splendid is the position of the Greek Theatre that it cannot be missed by anyone visiting Taormina, even those who are in town for only perhaps a few hours. You really need the place almost to yourself for maximum appreciation, but on that first Sunday morning a Royal Caribbean cruise ship was anchored out in the bay and the early-rising Americans were already crawling all over the site. And *crawling* is I am sorry to say the right word. Most of them were of course elderly, and contrary to our Sorrento experience not especially mobile. The site *was* demanding on the legs, though we did wonder if their apparent lassitude might also be explained by their having left the Sorrento Palace before dawn that same morning! Passing through in numbered (badged) parties, they seemed ready to move on quite soon after arriving; but in the meantime they did rather get in the way of our group. Clearly most of them were simply "doing" the place, which for Americans can take next to no time. My wife and I (and others, too) vowed to return to the Greek Theatre on a quieter day.

Our guided tour had not yet exhausted its usefulness. We were taken next for pre-planned stops at a café and bar to sample a variety of nibbles and drinks (in the hope of course that we would make a habit of using these establishments throughout our holiday). That was all agreeable enough; but it also gave us a chance to chat again to those on our flight who were staying in other hotels, and to make new acquaintances. We found that word had spread of our bad experience at Manchester on the way out. In fact it had made us quite famous among the community of British visitors that week, and of course provided an immediate topic of conversation. Our new acquaintances became people to look out for on our leisurely strolls up and down the Corso Umberto most evenings. If you have one supposedly awful experience on a holiday, everyone somehow expects you to have more. You can almost find yourself inventing them.

Finally we were taken to an unexpected and altogether delightful place which became our favourite spot throughout our stay in Taormina, when we needed a little rest and tranquillity. This was the English Garden - so called because it was originally created by an eccentric English lady, Florence Trevelyan. Nowadays it's a memorial garden to those who died in the First World War, and has an appropriate monument. Also on display, somewhat more bizarrely, was a miniature submarine. More in keeping, but perhaps equally bizarre in their time, were a number of elaborate pagoda-like follies, created from pale rough stone and brick, with bits of rustic timber here and there. You could only scratch your head at them. They appeared to serve no useful purpose whatever, which made them all the more intriguing. On first entering the garden we heard a very rare sound indeed in that part of the world: the twittering of many birds. I thought for an exciting moment that we had stumbled upon the last refuge of the poor near-extinct wild birds of Italy, but then we came upon a large cage and saw that they were only budgerigars. There were also a few pigeons strutting about. They were unusually lean compared to those you see in city squares. A number of feral cats had also made the garden their home. They too looked scrawny, so that we wondered if the condition of these creatures represented an ecological balance;

but the cats appeared not to be even tempted. It was more evidence of the charmed lives of the pigeons of Italy!

Our favourite place in the garden, though, became the walled terrace. This ran along its full length, on the sunset side, and if the view was not so panoramic as that from the Greek Theatre, you had a perfect sighting of Etna. Set at intervals in a thick hedge, entwined with bougainvillea, were comfortable metal seats. These were rarely fully occupied, even when there was a cruise ship in town. Often we sat there resting from our walking exertions and enjoying the view for a half hour or so in the golden light of the late afternoon. When Etna's summit wasn't obscured by cloud you could often see wisps of white smoke. We had heard that smoke of a certain colour caused alarm - they said the locals watched the plume as attentively as Catholics in Rome for the choosing of a new pope watch for the Vatican smoke - but we never established for sure if the black or white kind was the supposed danger signal. I thought the man had said white, but that was the only kind we were seeing and no one was panicking. The postcards showed a snowcapped summit. During our stay we saw little snow up there, and you could interpret *that* as a danger sign, too. The time of year (only late September) was probably the decisive factor, however. With its gentle slopes and barely discernible (from below) central crater, Etna looked to be a much less angry volcano than Vesuvius. In fact it is nearly three times as high, which translated into volume terms suggests a much greater destructive power, even allowing for Vesuvius's missing top. Etna is also deceptive in that the lava can issue from many lesser craters around the cone as well as the obvious central one. It is in short an extremely dangerous mountain, which dominates in every sense the eastern side of the island. But thankfully the lava has never in recorded history reached Taormina, and despite much recent activity (there was a minor "explosion" only a few weeks before we arrived), is unlikely ever to do so. Sitting on the terrace of the English Garden, you could feel entirely secure and relaxed.

And opportunities for rest and relaxation were most definitely needed in Taormina. For the middle-aged and relatively unfit, it can be a tiring place. We were confronted with this unavoidable fact each time we wanted to leave our hotel. Like many in the town, the Sirius is built into a steep hillside. To reach reception, we had the unusual experience of having to *ascend* five floors. In most respects it was an excellent establishment, but the lifts weren't altogether reliable. Most of the time they were both in fact functioning, but they had a disconcerting habit (certainly for someone like myself with an engineering background) of failing to meet the floors accurately. Had this failure been consistent you might not have worried (a mechanism should at least repeat itself with precision), but the gap *varied*. To be invited sometimes to step up or down as much as a foot into a lift could seem distinctly unsafe. Then there would be nothing for it but to climb the stairs - five flights. At that point you tended always to relax, forgetting there was worse to come. The reception area decor was pleasingly traditional, with period furniture and carpeting - a nice place to sit. It opened onto an inviting terrace with masses of flowers, potted and growing free. You stepped outdoors with a contented sigh, only to remember afresh that still facing you were yet more steps, now curving up to a sort of turning circle-cum-parking area, followed by a white-walled and bougainvillea-adorned length of winding, but also steeply ascending, private road. You reached the final exit at last with aching legs and silent groans, but then still had a walk of half a kilometre, all uphill, just to reach the *beginning* of the Corso Umberto - sometimes referred to as the main drag.

This lively pedestrianised thoroughfare, with its designer shops, pavement cafés and other tourist-geared attractions, which passes in a gentle curve through the heart of the town, is mercifully fairly level, making it ideal both for holiday browsers and the more serious native strollers, who appeared in their finery after dark. But all that can be imagined easily enough from the travel guides and holiday literature. As ever, we soon wanted to explore the less obviously commercialised parts of the town, and that meant many more upward gradients of one sort or another. This wandering had a partly practical purpose. Existing as it does on several levels, Taormina is a difficult place to get the hang of, geographically speaking. It can best be described as a three-dimensional maze. You might follow your directional instincts in order to get from one known place to another, only to find a steep cliff blocking your route. I would advise visitors to climb up to the Castello early in their stay. We left it till too near the end. From up there you can see much of the town spread out for easier understanding, as well as enjoy yet more magnificent views. You will grasp at once how the Greek Theatre relates to the English Garden (something that puzzled us for more than a week), and have an opportunity at least to begin to work out how a single road, specifically the Via Pirandello, can appear in so many different places.

The steps, rising from the Via Circonvallazione, climb in a zig-zag path ever upwards. They are attractively made in patterns of dark lava stone, red brick and pebbled areas, as you may notice on your frequent pauses. The low, flat-topped stone wall alongside makes a handy seat, and there will be others resting with whom you can chat. Being whacked out makes everyone surprisingly friendly. We talked to an elderly American couple (not I fancy cruise ship escapees) who were at great pains to explain that they were from St Louis, pronounced *Louiss*. Not that we had disputed the matter, but they had earlier spoken to another Englishman who happened to have an interest in Lindbergh's plane, The Spirit of St Louis. This had led to a lengthy discussion on how the name of their home town should be pronounced, leaving the Americans with the notion that *all* English people were seeking clarification on the matter. In fact we passed them on our way down. They had counted five hundred steps so far. We told them they still had about a third of the way to go. A little way below the castle is the Santuario Madonna della Rocca, which as the name suggests is carved into the rock itself. For non-Catholics, the tiny church at least offers blessed relief from the rigours of the climb, and would be especially welcome on a hot day.

Very early in an organised holiday you are apt to be pressed on which excursions you will wish to take. My wife was keen to visit the principal Aeolian Islands: Vulcano, Lipari and Stromboli. She hoped we might see the latter by night, when it was said sometimes to provide a spectacular firework display. An overnight stay would of course have been needed. Enquiries suggested that that would be very expensive. Then we heard from friends on the Via Umberto, who had done the daytime excursion, that the Stromboli volcano had looked quite lifeless to them, and furthermore that the smells surrounding Vulcano, where the presumably desperate go for supposedly rejuvenating sulphurous mud baths, were pretty unendurable. So we dropped that idea. A trip to Sicily might also be incomplete, we felt, without visits to the capital and largest city Palermo, and the nearby cathedral town of Monreale. But that excursion started at five-thirty in the morning and most of it would be spent in the coach, Sicily being a very big island. It didn't appeal, either. As for the possibility of a closer encounter with Etna, the weather was rather against it; and in any event access to the main crater had been prohibited since some French tourists had fallen in a few years before. ("Did they get out all right?" someone asked when we were being told all this!) I felt quite bad about missing that experience, at least for a moment or two, because deep down I knew I had in the past chickened out of my opportunities to look into the pulsating, cavernous soul of Vesuvius. But then Etna was a mightier and less docile beast! In the end we only signed up for two coach excursions: to Syracuse, and before that inland to the Alcantara Gorge and the town of Castiglione.

As usual it tends to be the minor incidents that stick in the mind. On the way to the Gorge, we sat behind a rather formidable middle-aged blonde German lady. Now, one can't help remarking that the Germans abroad are not always the most thoughtful and generally lovable of people. And true to form, alas, this powerful lady, who seemed to be travelling alone, decided without warning or consultation to tilt her seat back farther than was comfortable for the person sitting directly behind - namely my wife. Loud complaints had no effect, so my wife raised her knees and proceeded to push and hammer against the seat back. The woman endured this for a few moments, and then simply moved across to the seat in front of me, where she behaved more reasonably, though there was no attempt at communication. We forgot about her until we were down at the Gorge, noted for its remarkable rock formations and freezing cold river water. If you paddled you could make your way upstream a little, penetrating the more hidden parts. Rubber waders were available for hire up top, but most people, ourselves included, hadn't bothered. My wife dipped her toes in, before retreating to sit with her feet drawn up on a safe rock. Then our German friend strode into view.

She raised her skirts high and without a second's hesitation marched unflinchingly deep into the icy stream, passing with contempt several paddlers who were fumbling their way pathetically forward in their protective boots. All she needed to complete the image of a Wagnerian heroine was the horned helmet. After that display we treated her with the utmost respect!

The Alcantara Gorge was supposed to be the highlight of the day, but I found the town of Castiglione far more impressive - the first I had seen which seemed to have a life of its own not supported by tourism (although in truth visitors were passing through pretty frequently). It's one of a number of hilltop fortress towns close to Etna, created centuries ago by the Normans when they were the dominant force on the island. The view as we approached was stunning - but again I remember rather better another little moment of human interest. I got into conversation with our guide and asked him a trivial question about the prickly pears that were growing everywhere, which we couldn't recall seeing in such abundance in other parts of Italy. It didn't seem to make sense that they were being cultivated here and there, and were sold in the shops, when they were so readily available in the wild. Instead of answering, he told us how as a boy he had been given this fruit each Sunday by his father, as a special and apparently deeply meaningful treat. Everything he was and everything he possessed he said he owed to this man, who was now dead. We wondered and asked if perhaps he had been recently bereaved. He told us his father had died in 1972. Later in the holiday we happened at the end of another trip to observe him with his wife and children. It was very apparent that his love for them all was deep and everlasting.

Syracuse we visited towards the end of our first week. In its day - and it had a pretty long day - it was a Mediterranean city of enormous importance, surpassing even Athens in power and prestige for awhile. So many times was it occupied by new rulers that one wonders how the natives managed to hold on to a sense of identity. Evidence of this turbulent past is all around in great abundance, but of course for day trippers time is very limited. I find it increasingly easy, though, to go along with and indeed enjoy excursions of this kind, while remaining fully aware of their essential absurdity. You are taken to a few sites of special interest in a town or city, rapidly lectured to in several languages on arcane matters that you may scarcely have given a thought to before - then it's off to the next stop on the itinerary for more. But so what? say I. The coaches are comfortable, someone else has to think about the driving (no small relief in the Taormina area), and the little explanatory talks allow you to feel you now know *something* about the topic without the need for a lot of heavy reading. The guides can often be entertaining and stimulating, too, if you take the trouble to listen to them. It can all add up to pretty good value, in fact, if you're honest.

Much of the surviving older part of Syracuse is on the island of Ortigia, joined to the mainland by two bridges. We spilled from our coach close to one of these and joined our youthfully grey local guide. He wore shades, a medallion and fashionable jeans; but no one with a command of four languages should be instantly dismissed as a phoney. Nor was he in the least laid back. After the briefest of introductions we were marched through picturesque narrow streets to one of several squares on Ortigia, the Piazza Duomo. I had hoped we might first pause in the Piazza Archimede and learn a bit about the great mathematician and inventor, who spent most of his life in Syracuse; but he wasn't on today's agenda. Our attention was focused instead on the principal church. This building had been much modified in its long history by successive regimes. What made it unusual, we gathered, was that the various conquerors had been content to extend or modify what was there rather than feel they had to obliterate all traces of the past and begin anew, with the happy result that elements of each period remain in the fabric. Its cool interior and surviving Doric columns reflect its origins as a Greek temple. We were told that it had been converted into a church in the seventh century basically by knocking openings through the inner walls and using the stone to plug those in the outer. Certainly some of the masonry had a rough-hewn look about it. The present baroque facade was built by the Spanish in the late seventeenth century, after earthquake damage. They also did the present floor, I believe.

After lunch we were driven back through the city to the Parco Archeologico, passing *en route* a modern church that amounted to a huge upturned fluted and flanged cone. Judging by the number of times you saw its image, the locals were very proud of this creation. It would have been the despair of Mary McCarthy (though maybe she would have considered it progress). The Parco Archeologico had a Greek theatre, a lesser Roman arena, a dilapidated quarry and the celebrated Ear of Dionysus. Our guide wasted little time on the various legends associated with these remains - for instance that the fine ladies of the city had held perfume to their noses and been supported by their slaves as they gazed down upon the dead or dying Greek captives who had been abandoned in the quarry pit. He gave us instead a civil engineer's account of how the quarry had been worked. Similar treatment was accorded the Ear of Dionysus, a cave with unusual acoustic properties shaped something like a human ear, where the tyrant had supposedly imprisoned and eavesdropped upon his enemies. The shape of the cave merely reflected faults in the rock which the quarrymen had followed for convenience, we were assured. The place had in fact been given its name by the painter Caravaggio in comparatively recent times. Just before we entered, a party of Americans used the resonance to good effect in an impromptu chorus of "God Bless America!".

From Syracuse we headed north again, this time following the coast road and passing what seemed like a great number of oil refineries. They were something of an eyesore, but having earned my living in such industries for many years I was in no position to complain. On our earlier excursion to Castiglione we had been fascinated by the dark solidified evidence of Etna's many outpourings, ancient and modern, but it was nothing to compare with what we saw in and around Catania. The whole plain seemed to sit upon a vast bed of lava rock, the crusty edge of which formed the coastline. This plain is in fact green and highly fertile, though with a pervading darkness showing through. And the city itself is a dark place. We paused there briefly in the main *piazza*, alongside the Fontana dell'Elefante, a monument and symbol of the city featuring an elephant sculpted from lava, surmounted by a granite Egyptian obelisk. Through the opposite window was the cathedral, which again one gathered had been much modified and rebuilt as needed through its long history. Its baroque facade was totally obscured by scaffolding, but our coach guide gave us her full commentary without apparent revision, even so. Catania was partly covered by lava flows in 1669, then levelled by an earthquake twenty-four years later. Much of the rebuilding seems to have been in the convenient dark stone. Noticeable as you pass through the modern city are its many long straight avenues and lesser roads. Because it is somewhat off the tourist map, Catania exerted a strong pull.

In Castiglione a few days before, from a magnificent vantage point high above the Alcantara Valley looking across at the small towns of Francavilla and the partially hidden Motta Camastra (where scenes for *Godfather II* were filmed - almost as far from Corleone as it is possible to get without leaving the island), we had seen something unexpected: small flights of birds making their way down the valley. We had also heard the distant sound of gunshots, and presumed these were the survivors. Soon after that we telephoned the Menicaglis (as we invariably do when we are in Italy). Brenda told us that Roberto was out shooting. We knew better than to object, since we suspected that Brenda had gone native on this issue some considerable time ago. I have no special interest in birds, but one can't help siding with the underdog; so it was heartening to know that a few were managing to survive in that part of the world, if only to be shot at another day (though in both cases they were doubtless migratory rather than native species).

At dinner one evening I put this idea of the bird life of Italy being either extinct or close to it to our table companions, two non-academic gentleman friends from Oxford. They said it was funny I should say that, because they were being wakened by the twittering of birds most mornings. We hadn't yet heard them ourselves - but could Sicily be a special case? I knew the *mafiosi* had a reputation for kindness to children and wondered if this perhaps extended to certain kinds of wildlife. Musing on this very question late one afternoon in our hotel room, I happened to glance through the open doors leading to our terrace balcony - and there perched calmly on the iron railing was a *blackbird.* I hardly dared move, and almost expected it to *speak*, so improbable did it seem. Soon of course it flew off, but after that we began to see lots of birds. In fact there were nests all around the hotel, mainly under the balconies. They were highly visible and quite close at hand, so that you wondered how you could have missed them. What the birds were getting stirred up about, I'm not sure; but they began to appear towards dusk in large numbers, performing wild and spectacular aerobatics; sometimes coming in very close, then quickly retreating, going almost out to sea. I believe these particular birds were swifts (the first blackbird had been a lone individual). I might have been able to verify this had I been able to take any photographs. This was scarcely possible, however, partly owing to their rapid and unpredictable movements, but also because raising the camera caused them instantly to retreat into the far distance, almost as if it were a gun. In the single photograph I attempted only one very distant bird appears, and yet there had been *dozens* filling the sky. Although it was surely not the breeding season, they seemed to be mainly anxious about their nests; made as far as I could see from little stones, and roughly egg-shaped, with no obvious means of support. (I don't know what they were using for cement!) If I put the camera down, in no more than the blink of an eye they would fly in to inspect them, the lead bird briefly entering the nest, then just as quickly leaving it, while others, screeching and swooping, kept a close watch in what seemed like a state of great apprehension. I have no idea what was causing this behaviour. The most I can say by way of conclusion on this subject is that the birds in that part of the world, while not yet extinct, are certainly getting to be very neurotic!

Our second week approaching, we were very conscious of our failure so far to get out of Taormina on our own. The bus station was near to our hotel, so there was really no excuse for not taking at least a short trip. Our first was up to Castelmola. We knew it could be reached on foot, but the climb would be twice as far and twice as arduous as that up to the Castello, so we took the easy way. As on the drive to Anacapri two years before, I was somewhat intrigued as to how the driver would manage it, since no road was visible from below. It wasn't difficult to guess, however, that the route would take us around the hidden far side of the small mountain on which Castelmola is perched. Leaving the bus, we strolled along a few narrow paths and alleyways, and found ourselves in a charming little square. Partly perhaps because we were the first of the morning's visitors to reach it, we fell instantly in love with the place, much as had happened when we stepped ashore on Pescatori on Lake Maggiore. The fact that it obviously lived off tourism seemed similarly not to matter. We sat at a table drinking the local almond wine and enjoying the quiet moment before the few other bus passengers arrived. On the square was of course a church, in this case with a very plain rather than a baroque facade, but no worse for that. The priest at that moment stepped outside and crossed the square, giving the place a little extra authentic charm. But then he came back with a man who looked to be a building contractor. We watched as they began a quite animated discussion, the priest pointing to parts of the frontage, then stroking his chin and looking thoughtful. God knows what scheme they were hatching! Later we were surprised to notice a television satellite dish around the side of the church. We had a pleasant lunch up in Castelmola, then did the long downhill walk, surrounded by the kind of scenery that truly takes your breath away.

That was all delightful, so next morning we took a bus to the more distant but still visible Forza D'Agro. Waiting for the bus, we had found ourselves in conversation with a middle-aged couple from Scotland. The lady had taken up Italian quite late, but with such resolution that she was now not only completely fluent but had moved on to teaching it. She was another who had visited Italy many times and seldom went anywhere else. With her strong grasp of the language, though, she had become far more of an expert on things Italian than we were. In fact I am sorry to say that her knowledge of the country seemed to have become her only subject, and if you ventured an opinion of your own it was either ignored or corrected. A little knowledge may be a dangerous thing, but a surfeit can certainly be pretty tedious for others. We gathered that she was actually English. It was her husband who was Scottish, but she so dominated the conversation that we only found that out after we reached our destination. Forza d'Agro turned out to be a sad disappointment - probably, it has to be said, because it wasn't getting its fair share of tourists. The bus service may have been responsible for this: the timetable was arranged so that you had to decide whether to spend about three quarters of an hour there, or nearly *six*. And it wasn't difficult to see which the few visitors to the place in late September were choosing. The town had an incomparable position, and an enormous potential to attract people of the more intrepid and appreciative kind. To treat tourists in this way looked suicidal. Even the churches were shut up. Maybe it *was* partly the time of year, but there were more permanent signs of neglect. We saw houses in the more elevated and remote parts of the town that had been abandoned, and some you could see were being used as rubbish dumps. This kind of thing was sadly happening in other hilltop settlements, we had heard. The name *Forza d'Agro* was something to think about - "bitter power" it seems to mean. We neglected to ask our friendly expert in Italian to translate the name properly for us.

That excursion might have put us off further self-organised trips out, but we decided to try one more - by train to the small coastal towns just to the north of Catania: Acireale, Aci Trezza and Aci Castello. We had passed through them when returning from Syracuse and had thought they might be worth a second look. (It was difficult also to get away from the coast by train.) The area was being developed, we had been told, as the Riviera dei Ciclopi, the towns taking their names from Acis, a shepherd in Greek mythology slain by Polyphemus, chief of the Cylopes. (I had always thought of "Cyclops" as a solitary monster, but apparently not.) We took the bus to the station (miles away down on the coast) and the train to Acireale, hoping to walk from there south along the seashore, taking in the other "Acis", and then perhaps on into Catania again. It looked to be perfectly feasible according to the maps.

But stepping out of the station, we were puzzled to find that the seashore was not in sight. Instead we were on a long stretch of straight road, devoid of signs and with no end in sight either way. Knowing how inaccessible the Taormina station was, we did have the thought at that point that the Sicilians seemed to put their stations in some pretty stupid places; but we were still naive enough to imagine that we must simply have come out on the wrong side. So we went back in and tried again. But there *was* no far side exit. You either tossed a coin and started walking in whichever direction it suggested, along that uninviting stretch of road; or you took the next train back. That would have meant a very long wait, so we decided to give it a go.

It wasn't a normal road with buildings; instead it had high concrete walls or fences, and no footpaths. After about a kilometre we at last reached a junction, where we were able to cross the railway by footbridge and double back, aiming roughly for where we *might* have been had it been possible to leave the station on the far side. But we noticed that we were now entering a very shabby and possibly dangerous area. It looked suspiciously like the *wholesale* district; leastways there were no conventional shops. Our situation suddenly struck us as pretty alarming. We were surely the only tourists for miles around, and we had wandered deep into the territory of the middlemen of Sicilian business life - hardly likely, we reasoned, to be the most friendly. But there was no easy way forward. We were effectively stranded between the railway and a major, uncrossable road. This was nothing at all like the leisurely stroll we had anticipated, along a well-kept promenade, with a stop somewhere nice for lunch along the way. It was time for a swift retreat. And nowhere on the way back could we find a shop even to buy bars of chocolate or cans of drink - not one at any rate that we dared enter. We hoped the station might just have a small buffet, but knew in our hearts that it wouldn't. And it didn't. With nearly two hours still to wait for a return train, taking us well into the afternoon, all we had to sustain us was a single packet of Polo mints. Hardship indeed!

Our romantic (not to say rose-tinted) view of Italy died for awhile in that inhospitable suburb of Acireale - though I should mention that we noticed on our return that there was in fact a bus stop at the station entrance. We didn't actually see any buses, but if they existed I'm sure they would have taken us to the more civilised parts of town, and led to an entirely satisfactory day out. Indeed, the immediate road system had probably been designed almost to *compel* visitors to take a bus or taxi. But we couldn't think of setting off again. That would have meant having to wait for a return train until early evening, and there was no way we wanted to be still hanging around in the place after dark.

But as with that long delay at Manchester airport, the experience had its positive side: it made us more than ever appreciative of the beauty of Taormina, and of the tourists (many of them German) whose spending helped sustain it. After a belated light lunch we sat in the English Garden for a bit, and soon our intoxication with all (or most) things Italian came flooding back.

We even began to consider the possibility of taking a train next morning in the other direction, north to Messina. But then we remembered that another friend on the Corso Umberto had put us off going there. He was a sprightly old soldier (we met a few) who had come to Sicily to revisit old battlegrounds briefly known during the war. On successive evenings over coffee he told us in instalments a long tale of gun emplacements in various towns along the coast, and of local families he and his comrades had got to know, and indeed in some cases helped keep alive, through the turmoil. Deep bonds had been formed, leading occasionally to marriage. A close buddy of his had returned to wed a local girl, and he himself had had letters from the girl's sister, which he had carefully preserved. His (English) wife had recently died and he had decided to try to make contact with this old flame, even though they were both now well into pensionable age. He had sent her a copy of one of her old letters and had spoken to her on the phone; but when you would think that neither had much to lose after so many years, she had declined to see him. He was still rather hoping for a phonecall at his hotel. In the meantime he was visiting the British war cemeteries, looking for the gravestones of old comrades and paying his final respects. One trip had been up to Messina, which he told us he hadn't liked at all.

So instead we signed up for another coach excursion before it was too late, choosing one which would at least be visiting places we hadn't heard of before we began to look into the guidebooks. Our route would take us south again towards Catania; then inland across the great fertile volcanic plain with its lemon and orange groves to the town of Caltagirone (home of Sicily's ceramics industry); then a little way north to Piazza Armerina (to admire the Roman mosaics); and finally to Enna (a town with a commanding position said to be at precisely the geographical centre of Sicily). We preferred this itinerary to a visit to the more famous temples of Agrigento, partly because we had heard their modern setting was rather poor, so that they looked better in the photographs.

Caltagirone, about which least fuss is made in the guidebooks, turned out to be the most impressive of these places - a substantial hilly city which I admired chiefly because it appeared to have a full, authentic existence of its own, and yet was solid and well-maintained. It looked to be populated entirely by old men, who stood around talking and leading their own lives, indifferent to the occasional coach-load of foreign visitors.

Caltagirone's most famous feature is a long flight of steps, decorated with blue and yellow tiles, leading up to the church of Santa Maria del Monte. What you don't realise until you try to walk up them, however, is that they were apparently designed for a race of giants (the Cyclopes, perhaps?), for each step is simply too wide and too high for the stride of ordinary humans. In the photographs a solitary climber is typically seen standing with feet together, contemplating without pleasure the next step up.

Piazza Armerina I remember chiefly because it seemed such a testing place for our driver. The Sicilian bus and coach drivers cope with the narrow roads, steep gradients and impossible bends with such extraordinary skill that even at the end of a service bus trip you had an impulse to give the man a tip. At the Roman hunting lodge where the mosaics were to be viewed there were about thirty coaches occupying a painfully restricted access road. One was heading slowly in our direction, but our guide jumped down and insisted the other driver back up again. His command was heeded without protest, making you wonder again about the importance of having the right affiliations in Sicily. Inside, under a plastic roof, wooden platforms allowed a snaking stream of visitors to look down on the exhibits as they shuffled along. I have usually been underwhelmed by mosaics, and it was the same with these. Roman art is apt to be pretty lifeless to begin with, and making pictures from little bits of coloured stone hardly allows the artist to put much feeling into his creations, even when depicting scenes of savagery, such as we saw here. As I rather anticipated, they looked more interesting - and certainly more colourful - in the guidebooks.

Enna we reached with signs of a bad storm brewing in the west. We were taken only to the Castello di Lombardia, where we climbed the tower from which it is possible on a clear day to see all of the island's mountain ranges, though we could only just make out the neighbouring hilltop town of Calascibetta. Then we scuttled back east ahead of the storm along the *autostrada*, through an attractive landscape varying from barren yellow to lush green, the sinking sun now and then breaking through behind and catching the hilltops. But everyone was dog-tired and falling asleep. Even our driver was nodding at times, though he had more excuse than most.

Although the weather was generally fine, and indeed hot when the sun was out, we had had more rain in those two weeks than England had seen all summer. None of it compared, though, to the storms that night. The thunder and sheet lightning lasted for hours, and there was still heavy rain about well into next morning. It seemed our final day in Taormina might have to be spent in our hotel; but then in the early afternoon the sun at last appeared again, giving us a final lift. And we had a wonderful afternoon. Although the town has many highly inviting restaurants, we had not always been lucky with our midday meals. This time, however, we chose well. Then we decided to pay a last visit to the Greek Theatre, hoping amongst other things to take some better photographs. For once the amphitheatre was almost deserted. And we happened to arrive at the right moment for another reason: the light was just then falling on the surrounding landscape, and particularly the rocky escarpments, to very best advantage. A half hour later and the relief would have disappeared into shadow, a priceless moment lost. Next we decided to scramble down the thousand steps to a little restaurant on the beach at Isola Bella, where we had once or twice had coffee and almond wine. We found down there that the storm had still not altogether abated, so that great breakers were crashing in almost at our feet. Then finally we took the *funivia* back up to the high town and headed for the terrace of the English Garden, to catch again the golden light of the late afternoon and wait for sunset and a last photograph of the mighty Mount Etna. And that more or less concluded our Sicilian experience. It may not seem much - it's hard for me to tell for sure. I can only say that it seemed pretty splendid to us.

It also concludes this memoir of our good times on the Italian peninsula and islands, except to mention an old Sicilian lady who sat next to me on the plane flying home. She was all in black and seemed lost and bewildered, as if she was there by mistake. She couldn't quite believe that they would bring her food and had a handy hunk of bread tucked out of sight, from which she took a bite when she thought no one was watching. Then she would rummage through the stuff in the pocket on the back of the seat in front - looking perhaps for a sick-bag, we rather feared. And all the time she was apparently on the verge of standing to go to the toilet, but in fact only did so (I'm sure it wasn't intentional) at the most inconvenient times. Sitting on an aeroplane on her way to Manchester, with a difficult transfer to face at Gatwick, she seemed as improbable as that blackbird which had appeared from nowhere on the railing of our hotel room balcony. I took her as some kind of reproof - for the fact that consistently throughout this book I have shown myself to be far more interested in Italy as a place - even as an abstract idea - than in the lives of its ordinary people. This was the closest I had ever been, certainly for a sustained period, to an authentic native; but I had at my disposal little more than a few words of phrasebook Italian to offer by way of reassurance. When the food arrived she had some difficulty coping with the packaging, so I was able at least to help with that. I have no idea how she managed alone through Gatwick (it was difficult enough for us), but she was there on the transfer up to Manchester. Our prearranged taxi was late, so that we had to wait some time in the arrivals lounge. Whoever was meeting the old lady hadn't yet turned up, either. I don't think she had been abandoned altogether by the airport staff, for someone had fixed her up with a wheelchair; but for the present she had been left to sit in the midst of a swirling crowd of people. She was still there when our taxi finally arrived and swept us away.